WILTON
MANORS

WILTON MANORS

FROM FARMING COMMUNITY TO URBAN VILLAGE

BY BENJAMIN B. LITTLE

WITH THE WILTON MANORS HISTORICAL SOCIETY

THE
History
PRESS

Published by The History Press
Charleston, SC 29403
www.historypress.net

Front cover: Adapted from the watercolor painting *Richardson Manor House* by noted Florida artist Toni Sailor. *Courtesy of the Wilton Manors Historical Society.*

Back cover: Winter fruits and vegetables waiting to be shipped to market and the Colohatcher Woman's Club, circa 1924, from a Broward County Tourist Brochure. *Broward County Historical Commision-WMHS;* The North Fork of the Middle River at Northwest Sixth Avenue. Whms-Little.

First published 2011

ISBN 978-1-5402-3091-1

Library of Congress Cataloging-in-Publication Data

Little, Benjamin B.
Wilton Manors : from farming community to urban village / Benjamin B. Little, with the Wilton Manors Historical Society.
p. cm.
Includes bibliographical references and index.
ISBN 978-1-60949-437-7
1. Wilton Manors (Fla.)--History. 2. Wilton Manors (Fla.)--Social conditions. 3. Wilton Manors (Fla.)--Economic conditions. 4. Social change--Florida--Wilton Manors--History.
5. Economic development--Florida--Wilton Manors--History. I. Wilton Manors Historical Society. II. Title.
F319.W55L58 2011
975.9'35--dc23
2011032575

CONTENTS

PREFACE

In 1997, the City of Wilton Manors commissioned Stuart McIver, well-known Broward County, Florida writer and historian, to write *The Island City: The Story of Wilton Manors.* The city published it in conjunction with its fiftieth birthday celebration.

Accomplished author Cynthia Thuma updated McIver's work in 2005. This history greatly expands on that unpublished effort, using interviews recorded as part of the U.S. bicentennial effort in the 1970s, numerous interviews of people newly found by the historical society, the digital archives of the *Sun-Sentinel,* period newspapers donated to the society and important archives now available on the Internet from various universities, historical organizations and Google Books.

Among other contributions, Mary Gayle Ulm researched the physical growth of the city and made it intelligible. She is also the historical society's primary interviewer of residents and former residents who have stories to relate about our past.

The most important addition to McIver's work comes from the extraordinary generosity of many past and present Wilton Manors residents who have shared their memories and experiences.

WILTON MANORS MAP

This map will assist the reader who is not familiar with Wilton Manors in identifying important landmarks mentioned in the narrative.

The current boundaries of Wilton Manors are the North and South Forks of the Middle River. The Middle River forks at the eastern tip of Wilton Manors, and the two forks join again at the western tip. The city of Fort Lauderdale is to the east, south and west. The city of Oakland Park is to the north.

Just beyond the eastern tip of the city is U.S. Route 1. Just beyond the western tip of the city is Interstate 95.

Willingham's magnificent Entrance Gates were at Five Points, at the north end of the heart of Willingham's vision: Wilton Boulevard.

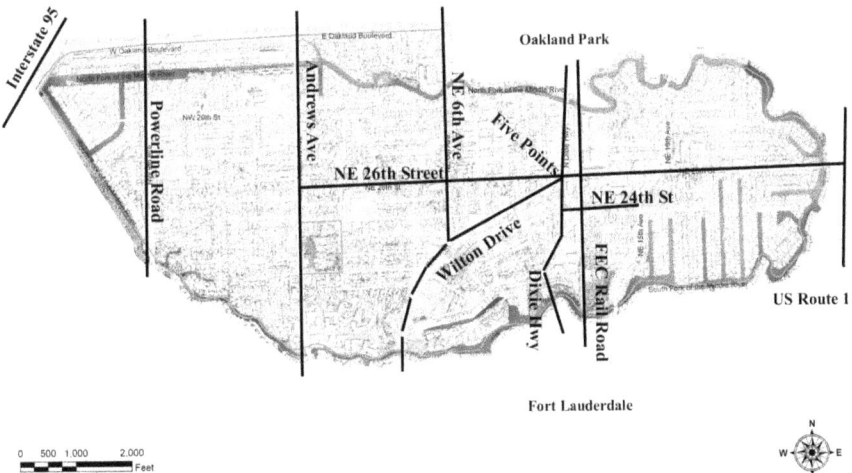

Wilton Manors important landmarks. *WMHS, Little.*

INTRODUCTION

Wilton Manors is now a two-square-mile municipality with about twelve thousand residents, embraced by the North and South Forks of the Middle River, in Broward County, Florida. Wilton Manors started as a planned development in 1925. The community started earlier.

Wilton Manors cannot claim participation in any of Florida's spectacular or important adventures prior to World War II. Like many of the "building boom" subdivisions, it had a failure to launch. Brought to life in the 1940s and 1950s by a number of extraordinary small-town folks, Wilton Manors has evolved into a home more extraordinary than any of the pretentious developments around it.

From Wilton Manors, you can be at an international airport in twenty minutes or in downtown Fort Lauderdale in ten minutes. Cross one bridge and you are on U.S. Route 1 to Maine or Key West, and Interstate 95 is yards from Wilton Manors' western border. Twice a month, you can watch or participate in the governance of the city. You cannot attend a public event without running into one or two commissioners or the mayor.

This high degree of civic involvement has distinguished Wilton Manors. Neighborhood barbecues have helped to finance major municipal projects. Over the years, volunteer organizations have evolved to fill voids in services and to guide elected officials. Citizens with "pitchforks and torches" will show up at public meetings when they are unhappy. It may take a while, but they get their way. One may count on at least one serious controversy per decade.

"Embraced by the North and South Forks of the Middle River" may describe Wilton Manors' geographical location. In fact, it seems that the North and South Forks of the Middle River guard Wilton Manors to this day, protecting it, nurturing it and allowing it to achieve a greatness of its own.

BEFORE WILTON MANORS

Lake Side Sand Pine Preserve—what Wilton Manors would have looked like at the beginning of the twentieth century. *WMHS, Little.*

EARLY RESIDENTS

Seminole Indians were the first people to live in the area formed by the two forks of the Middle River. Tequesta artifacts have also been found in the area.

Seminole camps were located near the southern fork, not far from today's Federal Highway, and were here when William C. Collier arrived. Collier began raising oranges on the south bank of the North Fork of the Middle River, in roughly what is now Middle River Estates, in the early 1890s. The area became known as "Colohatchee." One story has it that the Indians liked Collier and his oranges so much that they named the area after him: "Collier at the River."

Collier had moved to Texas and Mexico from Alabama in the 1880s to raise cattle. His enterprise was wiped out by the Great Blizzard of 1888, and he found his way to Florida. His obituary in the *Fort Lauderdale Sentinel* on December 15, 1922, states, "He was a good man and was highly respected…and was well informed so was a good companion."

In 1892, George A. Farnham of Saratoga Springs, New York, bought forty-two acres on the North Fork of the Middle River from the Boston and Florida Atlantic Coast Land Company for $515.37. Farnham held the land until his death in 1925.

More settlers arrived in 1892, when the county road from Lantana, on the shore of Lake Worth, to Lemon City, on the shore of Biscayne Bay, was completed. Stagecoaches ran from Lantana to the New River in Fort Lauderdale and from there to Lemon City. At the New River, a ferry operated by Frank Stranahan carried passengers, freight and mail across the deepest crossing on the run. Two small bridges near today's Dixie Highway got stagecoaches across the Middle River.

Stranahan established a venue to trade with the Indians who lived on the New River and in the Everglades. In 1896, Henry Morrison Flagler put the ferry out of business by continuing his railroad from Palm Beach to the New River and then on to Miami. By the turn of the century, Fort Lauderdale, named for the fort commanded by Major William Lauderdale in 1838, was more successful than many of the little settlements that followed the railroad.

Stranahan bought farmland on the southeastern tip of Colohatchee, in what is now the Coral Point Subdivision. In 1900, he married Ivy Cromartie, the community's first schoolteacher. Years later, she reminisced to a *Miami Herald* reporter about their farm:

We'd go out to the farm in a buggy or a canoe. It was a beautiful trip by water. Both New River and Middle River were very clear, and we could see tropical fish of all colors swimming around under the canoe. There was lots of wildlife along the banks.

Alligators, she said, sunned themselves by the rivers, and wildcats and bears roamed the neighborhood. An eagle kept a nest in a tall pine tree within sight of their farm. "I frequently made trips at night along the paths," she said, "but I always carried a lantern. The animals were afraid of the light."

Near the farm, Seminoles cultivated coontie (*Zamia pumila*). Two large Indian camps were located near the forks of the river, just west of today's Federal Highway, U.S. Route 1.

The Seminole name "Colohatchee" generally referred to the area from where the Fort Lauderdale High School now stands (Northeast Sixteenth Street in Fort Lauderdale) north to what is now Commercial Boulevard in Oakland Park and west to Powerline Road. The entire area was devoted to farming and was sparsely populated. This area was a wide portion of the coastal ridge that provided the eastern boundary to the Everglades and was suitable for growing heartier crops.

THE EVERGLADES

Depending on one's perspective, the Everglades were either an impenetrable, inhospitable swamp filled with disease-carrying insects and foul air that caused malaria and the occasional hostile native or an extremely fertile area, immorally going to waste. Approximately seven-eighths of what is now Broward County was "Everglades," the other eighth being pine land.

When Florida became a state in 1845, Florida officials started asking Washington for help in draining the Everglades so it could cash in on some of the agricultural wealth enjoyed by other parts of the country.

The eastern border of the Everglades was the Eastern Coastal Ridge, which takes a jog west in central Broward County. Most of Wilton Manors is located on the Eastern Coastal Ridge, which made it adequate farmland even before the draining of the Everglades began. Wilton Manors has been spared any significant flooding by all the hurricanes that have hit the area since 1926.

THE BOOM IS COMING: 1900–1920

By 1910, the population of Fort Lauderdale had grown to 143. When the town fathers realized that Dania, lying just to the south, was planning to annex their community, they moved quickly to incorporate in March 1911.

In October 1910, Frank Oliver, T.C. Moody and S.H. Weaver of Fort Lauderdale laid out a plat for a subdivision they called Colahatchee (with an "a," not an "o," in the second syllable), lying between the North and South Forks of the Middle River and running west from the Florida East Coast (FEC) Railway tracks to about Northeast Sixth Avenue. A note on the plat indicates that a mile west lay the Everglades.[1]

In April 1911, George M. Phippen platted a subdivision east of the FEC tracks called Colahatchee (again with an "a"). It was very small, containing only twenty-four lots.

Despite these plats, the center of a small community appears to have been the intersection of the FEC tracks and Mahannah Road (Northeast Twenty-fourth Street).

Maude and Louis H. Smith had moved from Georgia to Mahannah Road (1225 Northeast Twenty-fourth Street), immediately east of the FEC tracks, in 1910.

In 1912, immediately west of the tracks on Mahannah Road, C. Willis "Uncle Billy" Johnson and his wife, Clara, built a home using three-inch Dade County pine for the floors. Uncle Billy farmed the land and operated a dairy. He also seems to have worked part time as a telegraph operator for the railroad. He bought the land from Oliver and it appears to have included much of the eastern portion of the Oliver, Moody and Weaver "Colahatchee Plat" of 1910. Motor vehicle records of the time show "Uncle Billy" driving a Chalmers five-seater, which would have been about two and a half times the price of a comparable Ford or Maxwell. George Lindsey, for whom there is no other reference, had a Grant, only slightly less expensive than a Chalmers, also in Colohatchee.

In 1913, the Dixie Highway, running roughly parallel to the Florida East Coast Railway tracks, was completed through Broward County, linking the area to the northern states. Described as "rocky, rough, full of potholes, narrow," it was the first major road opening up the southeast coast to the new conveyance: the automobile.

Charles Mahannah and his family moved from Iowa and established a thirty-five-acre farm, and later a dairy, east of the FEC tracks. In a 1982 interview with Cooper Kirk, Mahannah's son Mark[2] estimated that when he arrived at age ten, there might have been thirty or forty people in the area. He attended school in Fort Lauderdale, getting back and forth in a "school bus," which was a horse-drawn wagon driven at a very leisurely pace by a Mr. Bras.

In 1915, the G.T. Smith family had a house at what is now 1303 Northeast Twenty-third Street, just east of the tracks. The Colohatchee Woman's Club built a clubhouse, dedicated on Thanksgiving Day 1915, just west of the tracks on Mahannah Road on land donated by Uncle Billy Johnson. It was located south of Northeast Twenty-fourth Street[3] at the site where Equality Park is today. At some point, it moved north and became the Oakland Park Woman's Club.[4] Just south of the Woman's Club there was a two-story frame structure. The downstairs was a little general store. The proprietor, Mr. Phipps, and his wife and daughter lived upstairs in a three-room apartment.

Plats from 1910 and 1925, as well as numerous references, show a train station at Mahannah Road that would have served the local farmers and packinghouses in getting their produce to market.

The 1920 *Fort Lauderdale City Directory* lists about fifty people living in Colohatchee, "[a] small settlement (PO Fort Lauderdale)."[5] Most are listed as farmers. The Williams' Packing House and East Coast Growers Association, fruit packers, is listed, as is the Woman's Club, with Ella (Mrs. Charles S.) Mahannah as president.

Colohatchee

COLOHATCHEE is the first station three miles north of Ft. Lauderdale and within half a mile of the Southeastern Packing Plant. On either side of this hamlet is a small river where bass and sergeant play. These streams run through most beautiful scenery, with palms and pines overhung with masses of trailing gray moss.

Out from Colohatchee are many truck farms, from which are shipped carloads of winter vegetables and fruits; the packing sheds make an interesting place during the shipping season.

The Woman's Club at this village is very active, and the results accomplished by this band of women give evidence of the enterprise they have, and the spirit of co-operation in the promotion of their plans.

Free bus transportation is furnished by the school board for the children to the Ft. Lauderdale schools, where they enjoy every educational advantage.

From a Broward County tourism brochure, 1924. BCHC-WMHS.

The Southeast Packing Company built a meatpacking plant just north of the North Fork of the Middle River in Oakland Park in 1922. At some point, the Colohatchee station may have either been moved or rebuilt there.

Considerably west of the FEC tracks, Merle Craig (M.C.) Slagle bought twenty acres on the south shore of the North Fork of the Middle River from "old man [Dr. Leslie] Maxwell" for $4,500. Its eastern boundary was about Northeast Sixth Avenue. He subsequently purchased an additional ten acres.

In 1913, a move to create a new county, referred to as "Everglades County,"[6] from the north portion of Dade and the south part of Palm Beach Counties was defeated.[7] Miami was building an expensive port, but Broward residents saw the port at Fort Lauderdale as a better means of tapping the riches of the Everglades. They also wanted to avoid the expense of the Port of Miami. In 1915, their effort succeeded, and Broward County was formed, named in honor of Napoleon Bonaparte Broward. Broward was elected governor with a platform of "drain the Everglades and build the empire of the sun." Broward's drainage program began with a canal west of Fort Lauderdale in 1913, followed by the Hallandale Canal. The drainage program started to open up the fertile land of the Everglades to farming and subsequent development. Port Everglades, now one of the top container handling and cruise ship ports in the nation, followed in 1925.

By 1919, moviemakers were beginning to take advantage of the state's exotic, tropical settings. That year, many sequences of *The Firing Line*, starring the famous dancer and actress Irene Castle, were shot in the pinewoods near Colohatchee. Chemical torches illuminated night hunting scenes, giving the jungle "the appearance of a veritable fairyland," wrote a reporter for the *Fort Lauderdale Herald*. Based on a popular novel by Robert Chambers, the silent film was shot by the Famous Players–Lasky Corporation and directed by Charles Maigne.

FAILED ENTERPRISES

Many saw great potential for riches in the area at the turn of the century but failed to realize a profit from them. Just south of Wilton Manors were two failed initiatives.

Florida Fiber Company

The area immediately north of Fort Lauderdale showed promise in November 1890, when Duncan Upshaw Fletcher and a group of

Jacksonville, Florida investors bought 1,310 acres for $2,293.07 on the south side of the South Fork of the Middle River. Fletcher was the president of what has been called either the Jacksonville Fiber Company or the Florida Fiber Company. The plan was to grow sisal hemp for use in rope and other coarse textiles, as was being done at a great profit in both Mexico and the Bahamas.

The company did so poorly that in 1891, it petitioned Dade County for relief from a tax bill of $32.41. One of the company's main problems was lack of labor. The property was eventually sold to the Florida Fruit Lands Company.

Fletcher went on to be a very successful mayor of Jacksonville. In 1908, he defeated Governor Broward for the U.S. Senate, where he served five terms. In his fourth year in the Senate, he became a power to be reckoned with as chairman of the hearings on the sinking of the *Titanic*.[8]

"Dicky Bolles": Land Under Water

"Dicky" Bolles bought a half million acres from the state in Dade and Palm Beach Counties for two dollars an acre in December 1908. Most of this land was under water. The deal was that the state would spend half the money received from Bolles to drain the land that Bolles had just purchased. In the meantime, Bolles was free to resell it.

Richard "Dicky" J. Bolles and his Florida Fruit Lands Company's eager sales force, dubbed "swamp boomers" by the *New York World*, set out to do just that. In March 1911, they held a giant land auction in Fort Lauderdale. The sales literature called it "Tropical Paradise," "Promised Land" or "Land of Destiny."

Within one week, more than three thousand potential buyers or their agents were reported to have arrived via the Florida East Coast Railway and stayed in a tent city.

The "auction" was actually a giant land lottery.[9]

For $240, a buyer could purchase a surveyed and deeded lot in Progresso, just south of the South Fork of the Middle River, and a ten-acre piece of the soon-to-be-drained swamp. References were made by unhappy buyers to "buying land by the gallon."

Bolles was sued, but he settled and was allowed to keep the $1,400,000 already paid, provided he did not sell any additional land until it was above water. He was indicted but found to be "an honest man." His effective defense throughout was that state and federal officials, and numerous studies, insisted that the Everglades could and would be drained, which they eventually were.[10]

Bolles died in 1917, and with him went the proposed town of Progresso.

THE BOOM TAKES OFF: 1920–1926

To the other excesses following the War to End All Wars, Florida added "Florida Frenzy," an uncontrolled explosion of growth on the scale of the California Gold Rush, seventy years before. It was a boom and could only grow bigger. The *Fort Lauderdale Sentinel* of July 30, 1920, headlined, "Building Boom Started and Will Continue." Below the headline were four short articles profiling new homes that were being "rushed to completion as soon as possible."[11]

Real estate was sold, resold and sold again before the first transaction could be processed. Huge amounts of money were spent. John Lochrie built

Fort Lauderdale News, July 30, 1920. *WMHS*.

a house worth $75,000 (about $4 million in 2010 dollars) on the beach in Fort Lauderdale in 1924.

Winborn Joseph ("Windy Joe") Willingham, an auctioneer, had come to Fort Lauderdale from Macon, Georgia, in 1911 and sold land for Tom Bryan, one of Fort Lauderdale's most prominent leaders. He returned to Florida in the 1920s. In Pompano, he auctioned land at Pinehurst-by-the-Sea and sold land for Harry McNab east of what is now Federal Highway. The Great Florida Land Boom was rolling. Windy Joe's cousin, Edward John Willingham, also arrived in the area from Georgia.

EDWARD J. "NED" WILLINGHAM

Edward John Willingham was a formidable force in his hometown of Macon, Georgia. In 1882, at age twenty-one, he started a furniture manufacturing business. In the 1912 *Men of Mark*, he is reported as having 150,000 fruit trees, increasing by 25,000 a year. He was very successful shipping fruit north, primarily because he handled the shipping through his own agents in New York.[12]

Willingham was one of the founders of the Georgia Industrial Home in Macon, an orphanage and the Bibb National Bank.

Willingham came from a strong family. He was a deacon in the Baptist Church, as were four of his brothers, his father and six of his father's brothers. Both of his parents were college educated, as were all thirteen of their children.

Edward J. Willingham, circa 1912. *Google Books, Men of Mark.*

In Macon, Willingham led the fight for paving the city's streets and any number of civic endeavors from the city council. He was, apparently, urged to run for mayor but deferred.

Willingham's wife, the former Eula Felton, was an honors graduate of Wesleyan College. Her obituary says, "She was talented in music, and art, having received many diplomas in each."[13] She supported the Woman's Missionary Society and its mission in China. She was one of a group of women who organized Heimath Hall, a home for working girls, later taken over by the YWCA. She had also been a regent with the Daughters of the American Revolution.

In his early sixties, wealthy and successful, Willingham took off for Fort Lauderdale. Apparently, he took up residence in 1923, but there are records that he had purchased land in Lauderdale-by-the-Sea and Pompano as early as 1920.

Armed with a lot of money, Willingham joined for a time with Melvin I. Anglin, a contractor and realtor from Indiana and developer of Lauderdale-by-the-Sea.

Harry Kelsey, developer of Lake Park in Palm Beach County, sold Willingham the beachfront from what is now Hugh Taylor Birch State Park to Oakland Park Boulevard. He called it Lauderdale Beach. In 1923, he contracted with W.F. Morang & Son to be his exclusive sales agent for the Willingham properties on Lauderdale Beach and Wilton Manors. Vista Park, at Northeast Twenty-eighth Street and A-1-A, was given to Fort Lauderdale by Willingham.

Willingham was engaged in what was going on in Fort Lauderdale. In 1925, he was appointed to the first Planning and Zoning Board in Fort Lauderdale, along with Ivy Stranahan. This new board was a major step for Fort Lauderdale in getting its development under control.[14]

Charles Rodes was creating "finger isles" off Las Olas Boulevard, where every lot was on the water, allowing him to claim Fort Lauderdale to be the "Venice of America." Joseph Wesley Young was developing a very ambitious Hollywood-by-the-Sea. North of Fort Lauderdale, Pompano was also booming.

In 1924, Willingham bought Billy Johnson's farm just north of the South Fork of the Middle River and west of Dixie Highway. Willingham envisioned it as a suburb of the county seat. He planned at first to call it Willingham Park and then settled on Wilton Manors.

On March 9, 1925, Willingham bought an additional 120 acres from W.C. Kyle and his wife, Lucy, and Earl Henderson and his wife, Alta. They had purchased the land a year before, from the Model Land Company, and were probably speculators. The Model Land Company was Flagler's land company. He received grants of land from the State of Florida for miles of railway laid. Later, he purchased land from owners and farmers who had failed financially in the economic collapse of the late 1920s. The Model Land Company, and two sister companies, owned huge portions of southern Florida and were reselling manageable pieces to developers.

Willingham also bought land from Charles W. Oakes, W.S. Holloway and T.C. Moody, of the earlier Colohatchee plat.

UNIT 1 OF WILTON MANORS

All together, Willingham had assembled 345 acres of pineland, referred to later in his marketing materials as "wooded highland." Location was a major advantage. Positioned within the northern limits of Fort Lauderdale, it was relatively easy to reach by automobile along the new Dixie Highway and by train. There was one northbound and one southbound train a day—the "Steamway to Sunshine."

J.S. Rhine, a civil engineer, completed Willingham's plat, filed with the City of Fort Lauderdale in October 1925. In the plat, the subdivision extends west from Dixie Highway to today's Northeast Third Avenue and south from Prospect Road, today's Twenty-sixth Street, to the canal just north of the South Fork of the Middle River.

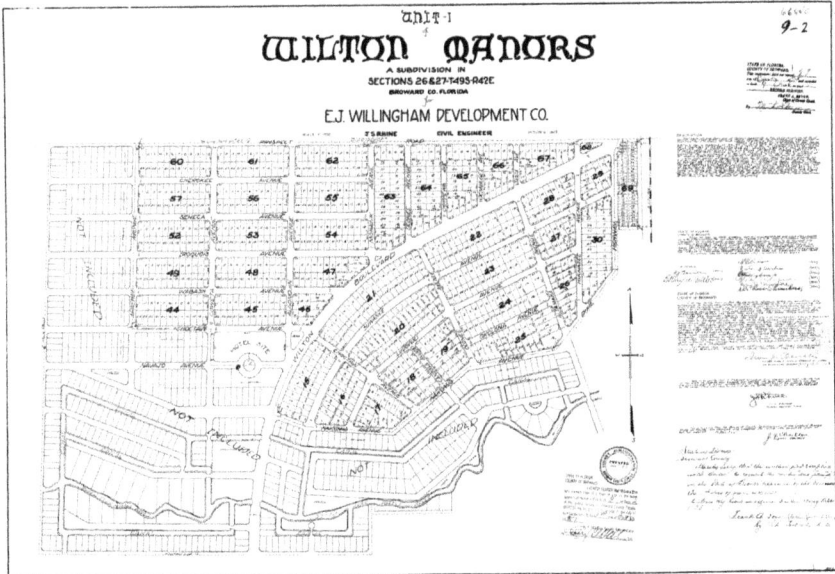

Unit 1 of Wilton Manors, 1925. *WMHS, Official Broward County Records.*

In 1925, when Willingham filed his plat, there were other signs of interest by developers within what are now the city limits. Plats were prepared for Beulaland, west of Andrews Avenue; Middle River Plaza, just east of the Florida East Coast Railway; Reid Terrace; and a plat registered by Max Swartz, also east of the FEC, all centered on County Road (Northeast Twenty-fourth Street).

The areas marked "Not Included" show a series of canals, touted in the sales brochure for the second unit: "Entrancing Middle River is to be widened and deepened for small pleasure craft." A canal runs parallel to Northeast Twenty-first Street, providing the north shore of what is now Townhouse Isle and extending across Wilton Drive almost to Andrews, where it loops south and bisects what are now Manor Grove and Richardson Park. This plan was never realized. The plat extends south of the South Fork of the Middle River into what is now Fort Lauderdale.

Willingham named the main street Wilton Boulevard. No business property was to be permitted on the boulevard, which was to be "exclusively residential"—and expensive. The street ran diagonally southwest from the intersection of Dixie Highway and Prospect Road (Northeast Twenty-sixth Street), creating Five Points, which became a central Broward County landmark. At the south end of Wilton Boulevard, Willingham built a twenty-six-foot-wide bridge (which he claimed was the state's widest) across the South Fork of the Middle River. Wilton Boulevard would be an impressive setting for the homes of the sure-to-follow successful entrepreneurs, like his home street of College Avenue in Macon, Georgia. Wilton Manors was to be very upscale.

Most of the streets with Indian names (like Algonquin, Nakomis, Mohawk and Okolona) were not named after Florida's Indian tribes. For example, Northeast Twenty-first Court was named Choctaw. Willingham named two other streets for rivers near Macon: Ocmulgee and Oconee. Though spelled incorrectly, Sewanee, a river that rises in South Georgia, also became the name of a street. Ludowici Avenue was named for a town in Georgia.

"A picturesque site has been reserved in the central portion of the development for a hotel that will, in all probability, be built in the very near future," claimed the brochure. Its location was to be on the west side of Wilton Boulevard and on the north side of Navajo Avenue (Northeast Twenty-first Street), occupying an entire block. The map in the brochure appears to indicate a plaza in front and commercial lots across the street. Subsequent development plans for Wilton Manors have also shown significant hotels, none of which was ever built.

To provide rock for roads, sidewalks and building foundations, Willingham's company excavated construction materials from a local rock pit. His publicity staff touted it as "some of the best rock to be found in the vicinity of Fort Lauderdale." The long-range strategy, declared the sales brochure, was eventually to convert the rock pit into "a beautiful lake, covering five acres of ground and attaining an average depth of 18 feet. This lake will provide ample facilities for swimming, boating, and other aquatic pleasures."

The rock pit became Lazy Lake, the area defined by Andrews Avenue, Northeast Twenty-fourth Street, Northeast First Avenue and Northeast Twenty-first Court, which is vigorously, to this day, a separate municipality.

Willingham's goal was to create "a high-class residential suburb" within a natural setting. "Blending with the splendor of the tropical sky and sub-tropical verdure," five parks—small green spaces, some of them along the river—were included in his plan. These were to be preserved "in perpetuity" for the residents. He established a nursery on the south side of the subdivision near the river for beautifying boulevards, streets and parks. The nursery would be available, too, for residents to acquire plantings for their own properties without cost. The nursery contained four thousand orange and grapefruit trees, as well as coconut and royal palms and shrubbery.

Willingham promised "complete public utilities—electricity and water from its own wells." Other "splendid" improvements would include fifteen miles of paved streets all thirty feet or wider, thirty miles of cement sidewalks, fifteen miles of white-way lights and thirty miles of parkways.

To put teeth in his vision for "a high-class residential suburb," there were restrictions:

Everyone was required to provide for his or her own sewage disposal.

Commercial development was confined to the east side of Dixie Highway south of Five Points (Block 69) and the little triangle on the west side of Five Points (Block 68). Hotels and apartment buildings could be located elsewhere.

A twenty-five-foot setback from the street and a six-foot setback from the side property line were required everywhere, except Blocks 68 and 69. The minimum price of a house that could be built on Wilton Boulevard ranged from $5,000 to $8,500, plus the cost of the land. Lots ranged from $3,000 to $7,500, fairly steep numbers for the time.

One could not build a garage or outbuilding prior to building the main structure.

All buildings, except gas stations, had to be at least two stories and constructed of fireproof materials, and there was a second mention of "sanitary dispositions of sewerage."

Then, of course:

> *It is understood and agreed that no lands in said subdivision shall be sold, leased or rented in any form or manner by any title, either legal or equitable, to any person or persons other than of the Caucasian race, or any firm or corporation of which any person or persons other than of the Caucasian race, shall be a member or stockholder.*

These restrictions expired on January 1, 1946.[15]

Willingham remodeled an existing house for himself on the south end of Wilton Boulevard. This would explain why it did not conform to his stated objectives of being fireproof. The house survived into the 1980s, having been the first home of George Richardson Sr. When George Richardson Jr. built his adjacent home, it became a residence for Richardson's in-laws. The house was part of the golf course complex. The third generation of Richardsons wanted to restore it, but it had sustained too much damage from termites, and bringing it up to code was not practical.

original 1920s art-deco
windows behind louvers

Photo of the north-facing front of the Willingham House taken in the 1940s. The windows of the main structure were pairs of inward-opening Art Deco casement windows. The louvered shutters in this view would have provided shade and air circulation, as well as screens to keep bugs out. There was a two-story porch structure on the east side. A 1930s photo of the ninth green of the golf course shows two huge palms in the front of the house and much lusher landscaping in the front of the house than either the 1920s or 1940s views. *WMHS, Richardson.*

WILTON MANORS' NAME

There are several stories about how Wilton Manors got its name. According to one story, Wilton was an ancient British branch of the Willinghams.[16] Another story claims that Wilton was the maiden name of Willingham's wife.[17] (It was actually Felton).

Most probably, Wilton combined "Willingham" and "Felton." "Manors" means "landed estates," but there has long been confusion about "Manor" versus "Manors." In 1956, Police Chief Beaney was quoted in a "Wilton Manors Topics" column in the *Fort Lauderdale News* railing about the Boy Scouts sporting shoulder stripes without the "s."[18]

As part of a fundraising drive by the Volunteer Fire Department, the city got its first Wilton Manors exclusive telephone directory in July 1957. The exchange was Logan. Most Wilton Manors phone numbers are still Logan-56.

In November 1956, Wilton Manors convinced the Florida Turnpike Authority that it should be included on its map.

Until the 1990s, it was common, particularly for businesses, to give their address as "Fort Lauderdale," as that city had more cachet outside Broward County. Wilton Manors shares five zip codes with Fort Lauderdale and Oakland Park, which adds to the confusion. Numerous efforts for a dedicated zip code have failed.

MONUMENTAL ENTRANCE: ARCHITECT FRANCIS ABREU

Willingham's commitment to his new development is clear with his choice of an architect to design the Wilton Manors entrance gate: Francis Luis Abreu (1896–1969), Fort Lauderdale's premier architect.

In the land boom of the 1920s, the prevailing architectural style along the Gold Coast was Mediterranean, drawing heavily on Spanish and Italian influences. The work of Palm Beach's Addison Mizner, the most famous of the Gold Coast architects, has been described as "Bastard-Spanish-Moorish-Romanesque-Gothic-Renaissance-Bull-Market-Damn-the-Expense style." The Fort Lauderdale newspapers of the early 1920s were filled with advertisements for Mizner's projects in Boca Raton.

Abreu was the son of owners of a Cuban sugar plantation who split their time between upstate New York and Cuba. Abreu graduated from Cornell University.

The Abreu family moved to Fort Lauderdale in the early 1920s. Francis joined them after graduating. One of his first commissions was a house for his wealthy grandfather, one of the first beachfront residences in Fort Lauderdale. Today, Jova House is the Casablanca Café. Abreu designed homes for his mother's friends. His obvious talent, well-connected family and gregarious nature helped him expand his business substantially. He also conducted a great deal of business on the golf links.

The Fort Lauderdale Municipal Casino and Pool, the Fort Lauderdale Country Club, the Dania Beach Hotel, the Maxwell Arcade and many beautiful homes, such as Marina Flores (now Rio Riente) and Magna Reva, are some of his accomplishments in Broward County.

A *Fort Lauderdale News* story, "Architect Working on Huge Plans," dated October 11, 1925, listed many of the buildings Abreu had "planned, designed, and drawn up the specifications for." The total value was said to be $3 million. Even if this figure were exaggerated, it is still very impressive. Listed in the third paragraph with miscellaneous buildings was "the field office, entrance gates and observation towers for Wilton Manors for E.J. Willingham, being designed in Italian Gothic, $50,000."

"The Gates," as they were first called, became the symbol of Wilton Manors. The larger pair of towers was located on the southeastern side of Wilton Boulevard. The second, smaller pair of towers was built on the northwest side of Wilton Boulevard, framing the entrance to Wilton Manors at Five Points. Archways provided passages for the sidewalks along Wilton

The towers at Five Points, showing the north end of Wilton Drive, circa 1946. *WMHS, King.*

Drive. They were constructed by Prescott and Boyd at an approximate cost of $12,000. The rock used in their construction came from the quarry at Lazy Lake. There was an "administration" building behind the west pair of towers about which little is known. Buildings presumed to be of comparable size were being built for about $20,000, which puts the total at about $32,000, not the $50,000 quoted in the *Fort Lauderdale News*. By 1929, it had become a school field trip destination.

ORIGIN OF THE GATEWAY TOWERS DESIGN

Newspapers of the time were anxious to make a connection between the towers and ancient Europe. The first reference found was in the *Fort Lauderdale News* of October 11, 1925, which described them as Italian Gothic. The eight-column announcement that Wilton Manors was "Almost Ready for Market" claimed that they were a "reproduction" of an original entrance to the Casa del Salinas in Salamanca, Spain. This was in January 1926. Two months later, on March 21, 1926, the towers were described as "having been modeled after the old 15th century Gateway to Toledo, Spain."

In fact, the Abreu towers in Wilton Manors do not seem to be "modeled after," "inspired by" or "evocative of" anything specific.

Connections to "important" places in Europe were part of the feverish marketing effort to lend credibility to the building boom. More likely than not, the Wilton Manors towers were an original design by a very young architect who was an astute marketer. It was common for architects to reinterpret all sorts of styles as "Revival."

The *Fort Lauderdale News* of March 21, 1926, contained a short article that, unlike other descriptions of the towers, seems to have been written from direct observation:

SHADED LIGHTS ENHANCE BEAUTY OF GATEWAYS

One of the most beautiful entrance-ways on the eastern coast of Florida, that at Wilton Manors, has been supplied with a splendid lighting system and is now a magnificent spectacle with its array of colored flood lights that shine upon it at night.

There are two towers that form the gates to Wilton Manors at the northern entrance to the property where Wilton Boulevard meets the East Dixie Highway. One tower rises 45 feet above the ground while the other attains a height of 25 feet. They are of impressive structure and design, having been modeled after the old 15th Century Gateway to Toledo, Spain, which has become famous throughout the Old World and America as "La Plerta [sic] del Sol"–"The Gateway of the Sun."

An indirect lighting system plays upon the towers from the outside, while from within lights shine through the vari-colored windows, giving an inspiring color effect. It is indeed a sight well worth seeing and this entrance-way to "Fort Lauderdale's Beauty Spot," as Wilton Manors is called, has brought much commendation from those who have seen it during the day as well as at night.

WILTON MANORS ALMOST READY FOR MARKET

Willingham, fighting a shortage of building materials, pushed hard to get his development opened in 1925. Finally, on January 30, 1926, the *Fort Lauderdale Sunday News* ran a story on the front page of its real estate

Fort Lauderdale Sunday News, January 30, 1926. WMHS, BCHC.

section: "Wilton Manors Almost Ready for Market." Smaller headlines told readers: "Development of E.J. Willingham to Be Marketed Soon" and "Manors Features Lofty Entrance Gate and 100-Foot Boulevard Which Shortens Route South."

There was a four-column-wide drawing of the entrance towers, "said to be one of the most outstanding features of the development."[19]

Other illustrations of the entrance towers showed cables strung between the towers supporting a banner that proclaimed, "Welcome to Wilton Manors." Photographs show decorative inserts of coquina rock.

The opening paragraph of the story read:

Advertisement for Wilton Manors, circa 1926. BCHC, WMHS.

Wilton Manors, described as being something new and different in suburban developments and destined to become one of the most beautiful residential areas in Florida, is the realization of the practical, yet unique vision of its developer, E.J. Willingham. The Manors consists of 345 acres of pine-clad land strategically set within the northern limits of Fort Lauderdale between the east and west Dixie Highways.

While the story made it clear that Wilton Manors' opening was near, wording implied that it might not yet be a *fait accompli*. In any event, the public was fast becoming less eager to buy.

Willingham, his right-hand man Perry Mickel and the sales staff used the towers as administrative and sales offices. A stairway to the top of the tall southeast tower gave salesmen the opportunity to give prospective "home-seekers" a view of the community they hoped would rise from the pineland. It was a fine view, Mickel later said, but prospective buyers never got to see a bustling town.

On February 9, a full-page advertisement in the *Fort Lauderdale News* announced that the E.J. Willingham Development Co. was open for business.

In all of the company's advertisements, the artwork featured Abreu's drawings of the towers. The copy trumpeted:

> *Wilton Manors is already an established community—within the city limits of Fort Lauderdale—two miles north on the Dixie from the city's business district—where values must increase rapidly with the city's inevitable expansion to the north—exclusive, convenient, accessible—between the East and West Dixie Highways—next to the Florida East Coast Railroad—with the beautiful south fork of enchanting Middle River as its Southern Boundary—highly developed and extremely beautiful.*

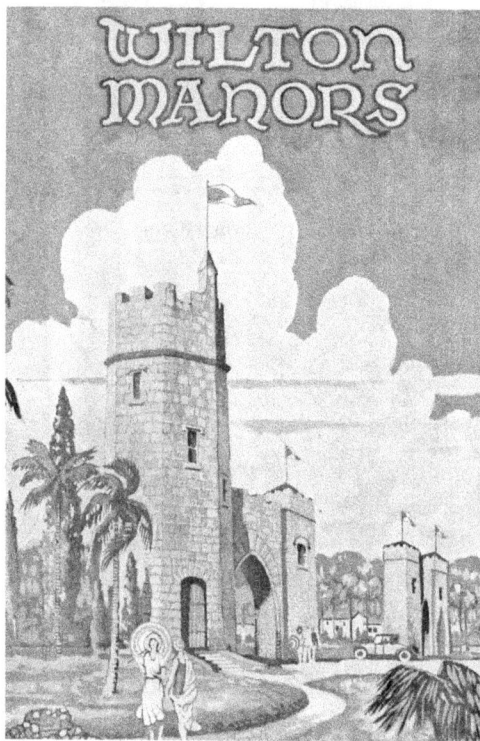

Willingham's sixteen-page color brochure, circa 1925. *BCHC.*

The ads, always tastefully presented, emphasized the theme of streets and roads. Wilton Boulevard was described as the new East Dixie Highway shortcut, eighty feet wide with ten-foot parkways on either side, eliminating seven turns on the old Dixie. The advertisements also claimed 11.25 miles of paved streets.

A beautiful multipage brochure with a watercolor cover depicted a pair of flappers walking in front of the towers. Photos inside showed the towers under construction and several houses. One of the houses was, in fact, the 1910 Louis Smith House on the other side of the FEC Railroad tracks from Wilton Manors. The others remain unidentified.

Before Wilton Manors

The company put forward an optimistic face on the project. Ads pointed out that even before the sales office opened, more than $250,000 worth of lots had been sold.

Early advertisements made overstated claims:

> *Wilton Manors is fast becoming populated. Seven homes are now being erected, some have been completed and two others were contracted for during the past week. Such settlement in an exclusive, restricted, residential community, combined with the excellent nature of improvements, means that values enhance accordingly. Here is an unusual opportunity!*

Probably the first house of Willingham's Wilton Manors was built in 1926 and belonged to Carl A. Hiaasen, a partner in the prominent law firm of McCune, Casey, Hiaasen and Fleming, which represented Willingham's company. The two-story house, at Choctaw and Ludowici (601 Northeast Twenty-first Court), is still standing.

In spite of all the hype, Hiaasen's house is the only extant house that to date has been confirmed to have been a product of Willingham's Wilton Manors. Willingham gave Hiaasen the land on which to build. In a 1984

Photo illustration of the Hiaasen House as it might have looked in 1925. *WMHS, Little.*

oral history, Hiaasen described Willingham as "a very religious man. He was a very imposing man. When he came into the room he was so imposing that you thought that Moses was there." He had a very deep voice, "but he didn't use it. He had a son who was very meek. Subjugated."[20]

Carl Hiaasen's name lives on through his grandson, also named Carl, a *Miami Herald* columnist who has emerged as one of Florida's and America's favorite novelists.

FAILURE TO LAUNCH

Willingham's project was doomed before it started. In October 1925, when the Abreu story ran about the $3 million backlog, the future still looked rosy. By New Year's Eve, the boom was dying. In the summer of 1925, the Internal Revenue Service had begun demanding tax payments on big-ticket sales—in cash. Speculators were in trouble because most of their profits were still on paper.

During the summer, the Florida East Coast Railway, overwhelmed by the crush of passengers and cargo, declared an embargo to catch up on railroad and rolling stock maintenance. The Fort Lauderdale newspapers were full of stories about the problem. Shipment of construction materials slowed to a stop by early winter as more than seven thousand southbound freight cars backed up at the Jacksonville yards. Meanwhile, the brigantine *Prinz Valdemar* sank in Government Cut, blocking the entrance to Miami's harbor and sealing off sea lanes into the busiest of the boom-time cities and ports.

By February 19, 1926, the Wilton Manors advertisements were growing smaller, featuring restrained themes such as "You owe it to yourself to investigate" and "Character makes value." By March 5, the advertisements had shrunk to half page. Eleven days later, the ads were two columns by four inches, using a soft-sell appeal to "discriminating home-seekers."

On March 7, the *Fort Lauderdale Sun*, a new daily newspaper, ran a Wilton Manors advertisement that demonstrated that Willingham knew the market had changed drastically. It noted:

> *Many real estate operators are beginning to realize that the hectic days of enormous profits have passed: that is also our belief.*
> *The conservative buyers who are satisfied with a safe and sane profit on their investment are the people we desire to interest in Wilton Manors.*

Before Wilton Manors

On April 10, 1926, the Willingham Development Company ran its final advertisement. The boom was over. The Great Depression that settled over the rest of the country in 1929 had arrived in South Florida by early 1926.

THE LAND BOOM AND BUST

The land boom in South Florida in the 1920s was a national event. Miami led the way, and Joseph Young was busy in Hollywood. Addison Mizner's development in Boca Raton was typical. Late on the scene was Floranada. The big draws were the weather and an opportunity to make a fortune.

Mizner arrived in Palm Beach in 1918, already an accomplished architect. His Mediterranean Revival style of architecture dominated buildings in Palm Beach, including mansions for the super rich and prestigious private clubs. He established Mizner Industries to supply cast stone window and door surrounds, furniture and lighting fixtures.

In 1925, he announced Boca Raton. Advertisements appeared almost at once in northern newspapers, touting the seemingly contradictory virtues of gilt-edge securities backed by the cream of industrial wealth and society and an opportunity to make a quick buck. It was heavily advertised in the Fort Lauderdale papers.

Throughout the summer of 1925, sales poured in, not only in Palm Beach and Miami but also to sales offices in Boston, Pittsburgh, Philadelphia, New York and Chicago. Others snatched land outside Boca and announced additional developments.

But the boom depended on having someone right behind each buyer, ready to pay more. By the summer of 1925, the fragility of the economic model was evident outside Florida. Key backers withdrew from Mizner's project.

Developer after developer and city after city defaulted on their bonds in the next several years. In January 1926, the American-British Improvement Corporation announced "the Floranada Club." Named for "Florida" and "Canada," it was to be the Biarritz of America. There were to be spectacular estates, casinos, a huge hotel and golf and yacht clubs, as well as "affordable housing" for those with impeccable social connections and not quite the obscene wealth that would otherwise be required. Backers included "super-rich" Americans; George II, the deposed king of Greece; and the Countess of Lauderdale.

Land for Floranada was assembled from Oakland Park and beachfront land owned by Arthur Galt.

By June 1928, Floranada had filed for bankruptcy.

It is said that Ned Willingham lost $3 million in Wilton Manors but paid all his bills in full. Others did not exit as gracefully.[21]

THE FINAL BLOW: THE 1926 HURRICANE

On September 18, 1926, a massive hurricane hit South Florida. In Broward County alone, the death toll reached forty-nine. Statewide, the toll was nearly four hundred. Willingham's home was badly damaged, but Wilton Manors, situated on the coastal ridge, sustained no flood damage. The land survived, but Ned Willingham's vision of Wilton Manors did not.

Throughout the area, businesses and banks were failing. The river of checkbook-carrying out-of-towners dried up. With no new money, earlier buyers could not turn their properties. They started defaulting on their payments, and properties reverted to developers who didn't want them. The tax man harvested land at pennies on the dollar.

Ned Willingham and his wife, Eula, returned to Macon, Georgia, leaving his properties in the hands of his son, E.J. Jr., and Perry Mickel. (It is unclear how much time, if any, Eula spent in Florida.)

Willingham suffered a stroke at his vacation home in Asheville, North Carolina, in the early fall of 1927. He died on March 31, 1928, at age sixty-six. Eula, who had been in poor health for almost a decade, had died in the home of her daughter, in Macon, on January 31, 1928, just after her sixty-fifth birthday. Their obituaries ran on the front page of the *Macon Telegraph*.

Booms are led by charismatic characters who become super villains when they fail. While other developers left investors high and dry, Ned Willingham made good. In a brief history of the town written for the *Wilton Manors Bulletin*, beginning in serial form in the July 12, 1951 issue, Norman Malcolm wrote: "Mayor [Dave] Turner, who knew Willingham well, said the latter always carried his check book along and paid on the spot. When the collapse came, nobody suffered by Willingham's defaults since there were none."[22]

By any measure, Willingham was a great man. His dalliance in real estate at the end of his life may have been a light dessert to his real work. He was a man of substantial moral and fiscal achievement in a time when these characteristics were not widespread.

PICKING UP THE PIECES

A month after his father died, E.J. Willingham Jr., administrator of the estate, filed an amended plat to Unit 1, Wilton Manors. The younger Willingham, whom Carl Hiaasen described as "subjugated" to his father, had been given complete power of attorney to buy or sell land in Broward County for a period of five years in 1924 by the principals of Wilton Manors, Inc.: Willingham Sr. and his wife; Willingham Jr. and his wife; and Willingham Jr.'s sister and brother-in-law, Mary and Ross Chambers.

In Willingham Jr.'s amended plat, the Willingham company relinquished to the public the responsibility for the maintenance of all parks, streets and alleys in the subdivision. At a time when the company had lost $3 million, this relieved the estate of a significant expense item. It also removed a portion of the property from the tax rolls—an additional cost break.

The amended plat removed the house lots and left mostly entire blocks, which were easier for subsequent developers to buy. There are notable exceptions. The north side of Northeast Twenty-third Street between Northeast Fifth and Sixth Avenues (a block west of Wilton Drive) remained divided into twelve lots. There were a number of others, scattered mostly around the edges. This may indicate, at a minimum, that the lots were sold to individuals. Homes may have been constructed on some of them.

The only other changes of note were the names of several of the streets. Perhaps reflecting more modest expectations, Wilton Boulevard simply became Wilton Drive. Streets on the west side of the subdivision were changed to create a system of numbered streets. For example, Choctaw Avenue became Northeast Twenty-first Court.

The plat, dated May 22, 1928, was signed by E.J. Jr.; his wife, Viola; his sister, Mary Willingham Chambers; and Mary's husband, W. Ross Chambers. The witnesses were attorneys C.H. Landefeld and Tom Fleming.

Less than six months after the death of the founder, another vicious storm struck South Florida, further discouraging outside investment. In September 1928, a sixty-mile-wide Category IV hurricane devastated Broward, Miami and Palm Beach Counties. Flooding near Lake Okeechobee to the north drove the final death toll to nearly two thousand.

Again, Wilton Manors held up well, but there was little other good news as the Depression deepened. At the Wilton Drive entrance, the towers stood vacant. Children playing in the empty building broke windows and set fires on the stairs. There were no prospective buyers or even anything that could be called Wilton Manors. Wilton Manors hit bottom when the company removed what remained of the stairs for the protection of the few residents and their children.

The Wilton Manors of the brochure was a gem. Ultimately, all Willingham left were the towers; the uniquely curved Wilton Boulevard, devoid of the stately homes like those on his home street of College Avenue in Macon, Georgia; and miles of sidewalks and streetlights, which would later be curiosities.

Willingham did, however, leave an environment that seemed to have the right ingredients for the community that would become Wilton Manors.

THE FOUNDING PIONEERS

The Kiwanis Club pancake breakfast at Hagen Park, circa mid-1950s. *WMHS.*

W ith the housing crash, the Depression and the onset of World War II, not much was happening in Wilton Manors. A couple of influential residents emerged in the late 1930s. Their number grew in the 1940s and 1950s. Most of them were farmers, developers, lawyers, entrepreneurs and housewives who bought and developed large tracts of land. They were the political and social leaders who made Wilton Manors a village (in 1947) and then a city (in 1953).

Typical of the era, very little was published in the newspapers about the contributions made by the women. The wives of the founding pioneers clearly made civic and social contributions to the growth of the city. A number of the wives had money and most probably provided start-up capital for their entrepreneurial husbands.

Some of the founding pioneers were business rivals. There were some personality conflicts. The village barbecues had to have been very exciting to outside observers.

With this group of players, Willingham's special piece of Broward County started to blossom.

John, Perry, Robert, Marianna and Dorothea Mickel, circa 1940. *WMHS, Mickel.*

PERRY AND DOROTHEA MICKEL

Born in Missouri in 1893, Perry Mickel served in the army in World War I. While living near Indianapolis, Indiana, he met and married Dorothea Applegate, a nurse, in the early 1920s. The newlyweds moved to Muncie, where Perry worked as a chef in a restaurant at a lakeside resort. When the restaurant failed, the Mickels moved to Fort Lauderdale in 1924. Dorothea had previously brought some patients for two-week visits to the Broward Hotel.

The buses bringing northerners to Hollywood, Florida, for the

The Founding Pioneers

budding land boom stopped at the restaurant Perry Mickel ran on Andrews Avenue at the New River in Fort Lauderdale. A tent city was built to accommodate the overflow of visitors. Perhaps seeing more of a future in real estate than in the restaurant business, Mickel went to work for Willingham, selling lots in Willingham's Lauderdale Beach subdivision. Mickel became Willingham's right-hand man.

In the summer of 1926, the Mickels built a garage apartment and laid the foundation for a house near the ocean. The September 18, 1926 hurricane struck the southeastern coast of Florida with winds of 140 miles per hour from southern Broward to Miami Counties. The Mickels huddled in their car and watched the winds destroy their apartment.

Even without the hurricane, they had had little chance to enjoy their beach apartment. During Prohibition, rumrunners began unloading their cargo on the beach. It was "too close for comfort," Perry Mickel said.

"We sold the beach house to the Capone gang, and they burned it later," Dorothea Mickel said. At Willingham's suggestion, the Mickels moved into Willingham's old home at 1937 Wilton Drive, which had fallen into disrepair. Troubles persisted. Citrus canker attacked the orange grove that ran from Andrews Avenue to Wilton Drive behind the home. The trees had to be uprooted and burned.

Perry Mickel bought some cows and farmed about twenty-five acres. Wilton Manors continued to be mostly farmland and woods. On a foggy morning in 1932, Mickel milked the cows and then watched them disappear into the mist as they crossed Wilton Drive. Suddenly, they came stampeding back home. Mickel discovered a pair of elephants strolling down Wilton Drive; a handler was sleeping on the back of one of them. Mickel learned the elephants had been taken from an overloaded trailer in West Palm Beach and were being walked to Miami, where they were to be featured in a circus.

During the Depression, many people in Fort Lauderdale lost their homes to foreclosure. Since Wilton Manors was a farming area, the effect may have been less severe. Perry Mickel continued to deliver milk to families in Progresso, across the river, even when there was little expectation that he would be paid. The children needed the milk, and malnutrition of schoolchildren was a serious problem. This was the impetus for Dorothea Mickel establishing the School Nurse Association of Broward County.[23] Dorothea provided for the family during the lean years by working in area hospitals and doing private duty.

In the early 1930s, the land north of the South Fork of the Middle River and east of Wilton Drive was sold for taxes. Mickel retrieved the land for the Willingham family by selling the house on Northeast Fifth Avenue to Frank Musebeck and the house at the entrance towers to George Smith, who owned a furniture store and a tire shop. He also rescued Willingham property in the Idylwyld section of Fort Lauderdale by insisting to attorney Tom Fleming that the bank that held the mortgage would discount it for even a small payment. Fleming was skeptical, but he came back beaming to tell Mickel, "My God, Perry, they took it." Mickel continued to expand his farm, acquiring additional acreage west of Andrews Avenue.

The Mickel family, including two sons and a daughter, eventually built and moved into their home on the corner of what are now Northwest Twenty-fifth Street and Northwest Third Avenue in 1938. In the late 1940s or early 1950s, Northwest Third Avenue was established. At some point during this time, the Mickel house was moved ninety degrees so that it now faces Northwest Twenty-fifth Street.

Perry Mickel was one of the founding members of the Civic Association in 1946 and became the second mayor in March 1952.

The bridge at the south end of Northeast Fifteenth Avenue into Fort Lauderdale is named for Perry Mickel.

In his later years, Mickel and his wife spent more of their time in Asheville, North Carolina. He died there in 1968.

Photo illustration of the Mickel House at Northwest Third Avenue and Northwest Twenty-fifth Street. It was later moved to face Northwest Twenty-fifth Street, circa 1946. *WMHS, Sawallis.*

GEORGE RICHARDSON SR. AND JR.

In 1938, Wilton Manors, Inc., Willingham's surviving company, sold George Richardson Sr., a native of Northern Ireland, "40 acres more or less" on the South Fork of the Middle River.

Richardson Sr. built courses for some of the most prominent golf course architects in America: Albert Warren Tillinghast, of Harington Park, New Jersey; and Donald Ross, of Pinehurst, North Carolina.

George and Rachel Richardson came to New York from Ireland when they were both in their twenties. George worked first in lawn maintenance and from that moved into golf course turf maintenance in 1918, the year their son, George Jr., was born in Rydel, Pennsylvania, near Philadelphia. His next move was into golf course construction, following the plans of the architects who designed them. He built courses in Detroit, Michigan, and Tarrytown, New York.

Building golf courses was labor intensive, employing as many as two hundred workers on a given project. Operating long before mechanized earth-moving equipment became available, Richardson worked with simple scoops drawn by mules or tractors. He built ten golf courses, in addition to the polo fields at Westbury, Long Island. Building a major golf course took about two years, so the Richardson family moved from city to city as each course was constructed.

The 1920s land boom drew him to Florida. In the mid-1920s, he constructed the course at Fort Lauderdale Country Club (now within the city limits of Plantation), for which Francis Abreu had designed the clubhouse. After he finished his work in Broward County, the

The Richardsons—George Sr., Rachel and George Jr.—circa 1946 at the golf course. *WMHS, Richardson.*

family moved north to build a course on Montauk Point, Long Island, for entrepreneur Carl Fisher, the developer of Miami Beach, the Indianapolis Motor Speedway and the Lincoln and Dixie Highway projects.

Each winter, the Richardson family returned to the Fort Lauderdale area. George Sr. saw it as an ideal place to retire. Rachel, meanwhile, had astutely invested in mortgages, so despite the Depression, the family could afford to move to Florida and combine George's career with retirement. "It was out in the boonies, out beyond Progresso," said George Jr.

George Richardson Sr. drew plans for a nine-hole course and then went north to complete a project. George Jr., who was eighteen at the time, and his mother began building the course to the elder Richardson's specifications. The southern boundary was the South Fork of the Middle River, and it extended from Wilton Drive to Andrews Avenue. They worked with a tractor and a scoop. Buddy Hicks worked with them to construct the course and was still working for the Richardson family six decades later.

The design called for a par-three eighth hole.

"Where are we going to put the green, George?" Rachel Richardson asked her son.

"I dropped a ball and hit an eight-iron about 150 yards," George Jr., recalled. "Where the ball stopped, that's where we put the green."

U. S. G. A. *Rules govern all play unless modified by the following:*

Local Rules

The roads on 6 and 9 are out of bounds. Penalty: loss of distance.

A ball may be lifted from the hole of a burrowing animal in hazard or fairway and dropped back one club length, without penalty.

A ball may be dropped back one club length from any drain-tile or water-plug anywhere on the course without penalty.

The ball may be lifted out of ditches on 2, 3, and 5 without the loss of a stroke.

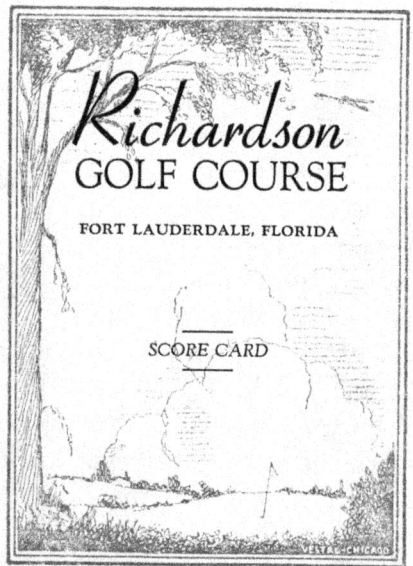

Richardson
GOLF COURSE

FORT LAUDERDALE, FLORIDA

SCORE CARD

Please Level Footprints in Sand Traps!

A Richardson Golf Course score card, circa 1939. *WMHS, Richardson.*

By December 1939, the course was ready for play: a 2,820-yard, nine-hole layout, with an eighteen-hole par of sixty-eight. The Richardsons built it without any debt.

At the time it opened, the Richardson Golf Course, which was closed in the summer, was one of only three golf courses in the area.

Winter visitors to the Lauderdale Beach Hotel and the Hillsboro Club were among the celebrities who played the Richardson Golf Course. They included opera singer and actress Gladys Swarthout; Ford C. Frick, commissioner of Major League Baseball from 1951 to 1965; and Homer Cummings, attorney general under Franklin D. Roosevelt.

"Our golf course anchored Wilton Manors in those days," George Richardson Jr. said. "I like to think it gave it a little forward motion."

George Richardson Jr. joined the army during World War II and served for three years. He then attended the University of Miami Law School. After graduating in 1951 at age thirty-three, George Jr. opened his law office in the golf course clubhouse. "I once got off a tractor out on the golf course to draw up a will," he said.

His father died in 1952. In 1953, George Jr. married Helen Williams, and they had three children: Kathryn (Kamie), George III and Gex.

Helen Williams Richardson was born in Fort Lauderdale and also attended the University of Miami. She was the daughter of Edwin Gex and Helen King Williams, co-proprietors of the famous Williams-McWilliams Ice Cream Parlor at Andrews Avenue and Broward Boulevard.

Helen met George Jr. through her brother Gex and his wife, Betty Williams, who started married life in an apartment across from the ninth green. Gex and Betty report looking out their apartment window one evening and seeing the green in motion; thousands of land crabs were marching from the golf course across Wilton Drive.[24] Obstacles on the golf course included sand traps, water features and crab holes.

George Jr. served as city attorney and on the city council. On January 28, 1968, Governor Claude Kirk appointed him as a Broward County judge. Two years later, Judge Richardson was appointed to the circuit court bench.

Alvar and Virginia Hagen

Alvar (Al) Hagen, single, retired in 1938 at age forty-one and moved from Berwyn, Illinois, to Miami and then to Fort Lauderdale. He "loafed" and played golf in his first three or four years in Florida.

Ginny and Al Hagen at a village barbecue, circa 1948.
WMHS, Woman's Club.

In 1941, he was playing golf at the Fort Lauderdale Country Club in a foursome that included Frank Muckerman, a wealthy Fort Lauderdale businessman. If Hagen won the round, Muckerman would sell his land in Wilton Manors, north of the Richardson Golf Course and west of Wilton Drive, to Hagen for $3,000. If Hagen lost, the price would be $6,000. Muckerman had bought these eight or nine acres for $3,000.

As Hagen related in an interview with the Wilton Manors Historical Society in 1975, this was "the biggest golf game in my life."

Hagen won the match and divided his newly acquired Wilton Manors property into lots. He hired contractor Clayton Leaver (whom he met through Muckerman) to build six houses at a cost of $500 each. Only two houses were built before Hagen and Leaver were drafted to serve in World War II. Hagen sold the first house to Ernie Johnson for $6,000 and lived in the second house, located at 2007 Northeast Fourth Avenue behind Wilton Drive.

In 1943, Hagen bought more than forty acres of land on the east side of Wilton Drive, from Northeast Twenty-first Court south to the Middle River and east almost to Dixie Highway.

Virginia (Ginny) and her family were vacationing in a rented house on Fort Lauderdale Beach. An acquaintance she met on the beach invited Ginny to a party given by Hagen's dentist. Hagen invited the women to his house in Wilton Manors. As Ginny put it, "Al had a car, and I had the gas coupons" during this era of war rationing. They were married in 1944 and had two daughters, Diane and Joyce.

After World War II, Hagen and Clayton Leaver formed the Tropical Homes Company. Hagen bought the land, and Leaver built the structures. Leaver owned the Tropical Construction Company.

Hagen and Leaver developed the property at 2000–08 Wilton Drive on the east side of Wilton Drive about 1946 or 1947. At the south end was

Williams Drugs, at 2000–02. At 2004 was the Manor Beauty Salon. Hagen's Tropical Homes office was at 2006. The Tropical Club was at the north end of the building, at 2008 Wilton Drive.

Hagen thought that the town needed a drugstore. He tried to interest a Mr. Moore, who had a drugstore in Fort Lauderdale. Moore failed to show up for two appointments, but Fred Williams, who worked for Moore, was interested.

Williams Drugs grand opening—Hagen, Turner and Williams, 1948. *WMHS.*

Hagen and Williams formed a fifty-fifty partnership in Williams Pharmacy at 2000 Wilton Drive. At the end of five years, "Doc" Williams wanted to go out on his own. Hagen bought him out, and "Doc" Williams opened a new drugstore in James Dean's new shopping center on Northeast Twenty-sixth Street. Alvar and Ginny ran the old drugstore for a while before selling it to an Ohio undertaker. He could not compete with "Doc" Williams, and it was eventually sold to a true pharmacist.

The Tropical Club, in its earliest days, was an important meeting place for the likes of the Civic Association. Over the years, there are various references to the use of this space. In a 1975 interview, Al Hagen said that the Tropical Club had a liquor store in front and a "poker room" in the rear. Hagen leased it to "two fellas from New York." Their intention was to put in slot machines in the back room. They fought, and Hagen took it over again.

Hagen's Tropical Homes office was next door at 2006 Wilton Drive. This was the advertised site of the "Big Meeting," where residents voted to incorporate as a village. It became the legal address of the Village of Wilton Manors until the new village hall was constructed on Northeast Twenty-sixth Street in 1949. It was also the first polling place.

The entire building is now Tropics Restaurant. About where Hagen Park is now, Hagen built a golf driving range.

For someone who had retired at age forty-one to play golf, Al Hagen had a very full second career.

A modern view of the Hagen House on "Hagen's Island." *WMHS, Jonathan Heller.*

Ginny Hagen was one of the founders of the Wilton Manors Woman's Club in 1948, the land for which had been donated by Hagen. She was very active in the civic life of Wilton Manors. Photos and the recollections of those who knew her suggest that she was a very beautiful and generous woman.

Willingham's original plat had suggested an island in the South Fork. Al Hagen made it buildable. In the newspaper article announcing "Townhouse Isle," it is referred to as "Hagen Island." Al and Ginny built their home at 500 Northeast Nineteenth Street, a very private lot on the water at one end of the island, in 1950.

Al Hagen also donated the land on which Hagen Park is located in 1953 and was the first president of the village council when Wilton Manors was incorporated in 1947. He continued to serve on the council until 1952 and on the zoning board into the 1970s. He played a significant role in organizing the first Wilton Manors Civic Association, which set the agenda for how the village was run in the early days.

CLAYTON AND LOUOMA LEAVER

Clayton R. Leaver became the most important early builder in Wilton Manors. He never served on the city council but was building inspector. He graduated from Yale and was a navy Seabee in World War II.

His parents had moved to Wilton Manors in the 1930s.

The younger Leaver's wife, Louoma ("Lou"), was very active with the Civic Association and the Woman's Club for half a century. She was elected to the Wilton Manors Election Board in the 1950s. The *Broward Sunday Sun* reported:

Clayton and Louoma Leaver, circa 1955. *WMHS.*

Much of the friendly atmosphere of the town is due to the catalytic influence of Louoma Leaver, who is unofficial public relations representative of the neighborhood. Her delightful name was chosen by her mother, from an Ohio River riverboat which passed back and forth before their home in Huntington, West Virginia.

Louoma offers true southern hospitality and friendliness to all who come to see for themselves the development of Wilton Manor [sic], and is responsible for many of its civic and social activities. Her pride in the development of the town, and in her husband's contribution to it, has had a great deal to do with the civic consciousness of Wilton Manor [sic].[25]

In 1947, Leaver opened the Tropical Construction Co. Very quickly, he became one of the first developers to begin building condominiums along the Intracoastal Waterway. He then expanded to building hotels, such as the Bahama Hotel, and warehouses along the East Coast.

For many years after her husband's death, Lou Leaver managed the couple's real estate holdings from an office in the strip shopping center at the southern end of Wilton Drive. She died in 2007, leaving no children. The large collection of contemporary newspapers left by Lou Leaver at her death has provided the historical society with important source material.

DAVE TURNER

Dave (not David) Turner moved to Wilton Manors with his family in 1945 and settled into a house he bought at 437 Northeast Twenty-second Street. He was born near St. Augustine in 1896. His father, Aden Waterman Turner, had been Broward County's first sheriff, from 1915 to 1922, and took up that role again from 1929 to 1933. After serving in World War I, Dave returned to operate Fort Lauderdale's branch of Hector Supply Company, a supplier of feed, fertilizer and other farm products.

About 1943, he bought out the Lauderdale branch and, a couple of years later, moved what was now Turner and Taylor Feed Store to Wilton Manors, near Five Points. Like his father, he moved into public service, in time becoming chairman of the Broward County Port Authority.

In 1945, when the original Willingham deed restrictions expired, Turner bought 283 lots from the Willingham estate in Wilton Manors for $12,500. With James Dean and others, he also platted the land east of the FEC Railway and south of Northeast Twenty-sixth Street. Turner was not a man who thought small. In his time, he became one of the largest private landowners in Florida, as well as the person who transformed Wilton Manors from a subdivision into a city.

Turner was the village of Wilton Manors' first mayor from 1947 to 1952. In 1955, he became the first president of the Wilton Manors National Bank. He donated the land for the village meeting hall,

Dave Turner, circa 1940s. *WMHS.*

which became the public library, and for the elementary school, both on Northeast Twenty-sixth Street. Governor Fuller Warren appointed him in 1949 as the first board chairman of the Central & Southern Flood Control District. He was appointed in 1953 by Governor Charley Johns to the State Road Board (SRB) as the representative for the southeastern district and was instrumental in getting six bridges built over the Intracoastal Waterway in Broward County. After he stepped down from the SRB, the state named one of those bridges in his honor: the Oakland Park Boulevard bridge over the Intracoastal Waterway.

Turner also served as Broward County port commissioner for seven years. His grandson, Bill Turner, served on the city council from 1982 to 1986, and his great-grandson became a Wilton Manors police officer in 2007. Dave Turner died at age eighty-three in 1980.

J. FRANK STARLING

J. Frank Starling crowns Joanne Zuffelato 1959's "Miss Wilton Manors." *WMHS.*

James Frank Starling came to Wilton Manors in 1946. Born in Key West, Florida, in 1918 and raised in Miami, he started out as a farmer and at one time cultivated more than one thousand acres in Pompano Beach and southern Palm Beach County, selling vegetables to northern markets. He served in the Army Air Corps in World War II and then became a lifelong member of the American Legion.

As one of the principals of Manor Market, he was elected as the "Businessmen's Candidate" to the Wilton Manors Council in March 1952. He served on the city council until November 1955, when, at age thirty-seven, he was elected as the third mayor of Wilton Manors and served until January 1960. In the 1955 race for mayor, he beat council member George Richardson Jr. by just seven votes.

Starling became the city's first city administrator on a temporary basis in 1960 and stayed on until his retirement in 1981. He served the entire time without a contract. While city administrator, Starling also held the positions of city clerk, treasurer, purchasing agent and elections supervisor. His salary was $23,530 in the late 1970s.

As city administrator, he supervised the organization of a growing city staff to meet the needs of a city that, by 1960, had a population of 8,257, an eightfold increase in ten years!

Starling and his first wife, Mary, had one daughter and lived at 2515 Northeast Sixth Avenue (around the corner from Manor Market). After Mary died, he remarried, and he and his second wife, Ethel, had a daughter and son. They resided at 501 Northeast Twenty-eighth Street. Starling died on November 13, 1995, at age seventy-seven. In honor of his twenty-nine years of public service, his funeral cortege drove past the Wilton Manors City Hall, where the city employees stood outside in tribute to his memory and contributions.

JOHN P. PEDERSEN

John P. Pedersen and his wife, Lillian, arrived in Wilton Manors from Racine, Wisconsin, after John, a builder, injured his back in a fall from a roof in the early 1940s. Stopping first in Tampa, they continued on to Wilton Manors. Initially, the Pedersens wintered in Wilton Manors and returned to Racine for the summer. Their two children, Jack and Shirley, did not attend school here because their parents did not want to pay fifteen dollars to register their car in Florida. Shirley reports that they attended the beach instead.

Some years before they arrived in Florida, Lillian had hit on the idea of making curtain tiebacks, and the project grew from a home-based business into a profitable operation. Her customers included Montgomery Ward and Sears and Roebuck. Although Lillian had only completed sixth grade and Pedersen, seventh grade, they were both very astute businesspeople.

Upon arrival in Florida, Pedersen began purchasing tax-delinquent property. He bought these properties on the Fort Lauderdale Courthouse steps for no more than eight or ten dollars a lot. He did not buy waterfront property, as it was too expensive—more than fifteen dollars a lot.

During the war, Pedersen could not purchase building materials for homes to build on the land he was purchasing. He could, however, purchase building materials to build chicken coops to support the war effort, which he did. At the end of the war, he threw out the chickens, cleaned up the coops, added kitchens, bedrooms and bathrooms and sold them as starter homes to returning soldiers and their families. At least two of these chicken coops remain, at 430 and 436 Northeast Twenty-first Court.

In 1943, the Pedersen family lived at 90 Northeast Twenty-first Court, and Pedersen had a business interest in the subdivision of Lazy Lake, across the street. Lazy Lake—to this

John Pedersen tending chickens at one of his chicken coops, 1940s. *WMHS, Pedersen.*

day not part of Wilton Manors—was platted in 1942. Lazy Lake was famously the quarry for the towers and a number of other structures, leaving a big hole in the ground, which was filled to create a lake. Pedersen thought it needed goldfish, so he dumped something in to kill what turned out to be many more than expected resident fish. Dorothea Mickel reports that the stench permeated the neighborhood. Pedersen tried to talk her boys into cleaning up the mess.

Modern view of the Pedersen House, built 1947. *WMHS, Little.*

Pedersen lived in several locations in Wilton Manors. Most spectacular is the home he built for himself at 2125 Northeast Fifth Avenue in 1947. His son Jack modified commercially available plans. The dining room's front wall is curved and all windows. The large living room sports a large fireplace, and there is a small atrium on the way to the backyard, where there was a little pool. There was no central air conditioning. Both Pedersen and his wife were fascinated by elegant movies, and much of the decoration was inspired by the glamour of Hollywood.

Not readily apparent to visitors were the one-way mirror from the master bedroom closet into the living room or the secret room behind the fireplace. The secret room held not only goods still in short supply after the war but also cash. Pedersen also buried cash in the little atrium. He built a larger replica of the house in Boca Raton.

Pedersen was in attendance at the "Big Meeting," where residents voted to incorporate as a village in 1947. The transcript indicates that Pedersen opposed it. Highland Estates and Lazy Lake had already been exempted. Pedersen was not enthusiastic about including some of his land. At the time, he was one of the largest private landholders in the Fort Lauderdale area and tremendously powerful. At one point, Colonel Robinson, moderator of the assembly, asked if Pedersen were threatening the meeting.

When asked if Pedersen had voted for or against incorporation, his daughter responded that he probably did not vote at all. She said he never voted because he thought that the Electoral College was a sham.[26]

In 1950, Pedersen found Mizner's 1926 "booming" Boca Raton, now a sleepy town of fewer than one thousand residents. He thought it would be the perfect locale for a wild animal park, where exotic animals roamed free in lush surroundings. He bought three hundred acres and sent his son Jack off to eastern Africa to acquire the animals. He returned with more animals than had ever been in a single boat shipment from Africa. Florida senator George Smathers was instrumental in clearing their arrival with the Everglades port authorities.

Pedersen's daughter Shirley and son-in-law George Schneider grew many of the fifty-five thousand plants needed for the park at the Schneiders' nursery at 2524 Northeast Fifth Avenue, where the Marvilla Condominium now stands.

The park became Africa, U.S.A. It predated Walt Disney's Wild Kingdom by eighteen years, and Disney was an admirer. There were a number of celebrity animals, including Princess Margaret, a baby chimpanzee that made numerous appearances on the Jack Paar television show. Princess Margaret was treated like one of the Pedersen children. She would kiss on command! Jack Paar and friends, such as Frank Sinatra, dined at the Pedersen home in Boca.

The park operated between 1953 and 1961, when Boca, which had grown prosperous following the success of Africa, U.S.A., crowded it out. The property is now the Camino Gardens subdivision.

Pedersen was focused and relentless. He had three objectives: to become a millionaire, to bring a piece of Africa to the United States and to live to be one hundred. He was more than a millionaire and created Africa, U.S.A. He died in 1996 in his 100th year.

JAMES DEAN

James C. Dean Jr. was born in Alabama in 1912. Dean's family moved to Georgia, and James graduated from the University of Georgia in 1935. He came to Miami Beach for a vacation in 1936 and stayed. He took a job as an insurance salesman for Gulf Life Insurance Company. By 1941, his sales territory covered Broward and Dade Counties and the Florida Keys. Dean enlisted in the Army Air Corps in 1943 and was sent to the South Pacific. He returned to Florida in 1945 and was named manager of Gulf Life Insurance, Fort Lauderdale Office. He met his future wife, LaWayne, in Miami, and they were married in 1946.

The Deans purchased two lots and had a home built at 701 Wilton Drive. They moved into their home in March 1947. It was torn down in 2005 to make way for the starkly modern Island City Lofts.

In August 1953, Dean announced the construction of the Manor Gate Shopping Center. His plan was to build, over a five- to seven-year period, twenty-three stores and a movie theater, bank and city hall on a fifteen-acre tract covering both sides of Northeast Twenty-sixth Street just east of Five Points. The anchor point was to be a ten-story office building with a rooftop restaurant.

James C. Dean, circa 1950s. *WMHS.*

Plans Unveiled for Huge Wilton Center

Dean's Manor Gate design, *Miami Herald*, August 16, 1953. *WMHS.*

"I showed the drawing to Dwight Rodgers—he was my attorney," Dean said. "He told me, 'Take the word bank off there. You'll never get a bank out there in all those palmettos and pine trees.' I told him to just wait and see. We were going to get a bank, and if he was interested, I'd like to have him on the board of directors."

Manor Gate was not built as advertised. While Dean may have been a loud proponent of a bank, the Wilton Manors National Bank was founded by Clay D. Dyal Jr., son of an Orlando banker. The bank wound up on the north side of the street, and an A&P Supermarket was the anchor store of the shopping center. The A&P is now the local landmark Old Florida Seafood House.

Dean and Turner offered to donate land to the city to build a new city hall here, but they were rebuffed by businessmen who did not want to shift the focus of "downtown" from Wilton Drive.

Dean played a very active role in the development of Wilton Manors, particularly the area east of the FEC tracks. He worked through "holding companies," and his name appears only infrequently with these enterprises. He joined many organizations, serving on the board of directors of several. As president of the village council, he carried the Articles of Incorporation to Tallahassee to make Wilton Manors a city in 1953.

The Founding Pioneers

In the mid-1950s, Dean, Turner and a Fort Lauderdale entrepreneur named C. Robert Clark ventured to the west coast of Florida, just south of Tampa, for a $10 million project with the vision of creating Tampa Beach, the prototypical new Florida city. The six thousand acres and the task of creating the Flamingo Canal proved too much for them. They returned to Wilton Manors. "Tampa Beach" is now Apollo Beach. Curiously, local Tampa history describes Turner, Dean and Clark as bumpkins from New York. It is unclear how they were saddled with the epithet "from New York," but carving a city out of swamp and building drainage canals was a great deal more complex than cajoling fellow businessmen into building a road and a bridge.

In 1958, Dean formed Gold Coast Broadcasters, Inc., builders and owners of radio station WPOM in Fort Lauderdale. Dean was also one of the founders of Broward General Hospital.

LaWayne Chaplin Dean was born in Zephyrhills, Florida, in 1923. She saw service during World War II as a WAVE. After their marriage in 1946, they honeymooned in Havana. Their five children were all born in the house on Wilton Drive, and she spent much of her time raising them. From Wilton Drive, they moved to Coral Gardens Drive. Neighbors report that Dean took loving and patient care of LaWayne in her final days, taking her for daily walks, which grew shorter as her health failed.

Dean died on December 11, 2006, just four days shy of his ninety-fifth birthday.

WILLIAM G. MILLER JR.

William Miller, a graduate of the University of Florida, was admitted to the bar in 1950. In 1952, he was hired by the Village of Wilton Manors to be its attorney. He served in this position for thirty years, until 1982.

Miller's family moved to Fort Lauderdale in 1926, when Bill was a year old. His boyhood friend, Odell Hiaasen, son of attorney Carl Hiassen, lived in Wilton Manors. They often fished at Lazy Lake.

Bill met Pat Breslin at the University of Florida, and they were married in January 1947. Bill and Pat returned to South Florida in 1951, and Bill joined his father's law firm. They built a home at what is now 732 Northwest Twenty-second Street. The house was designed by Pat's uncle, prominent Fort Lauderdale architect Don Macneir, and built by Perry Mickel and his son Bob in 1955. For many years Wilton Manors residents flocked to

William G. Miller, circa 1953. *WMHS, Miller.*

the Miller home during the holiday season to view the live eighteen-foot Christmas tree Bill Miller had shipped in for the enjoyment of his family and friends.

Miller drafted a charter to make Wilton Manors a city, and Miller's secretary, Alicia Zachman, typed the fifty-five-page Articles of Incorporation on an L.C. Smith manual typewriter. Zachman later attended law school, served as assistant city attorney for twelve years and became a partner in Miller's private law firm. Miller and village council president James Dean carried the Articles of Incorporation to Tallahassee in 1953. They successfully lobbied the state legislature, and Wilton Manors transitioned from a "village" to a "city" on June 4, 1953.

Miller guided the new city through the intricacies of securing the first bond issue for sewers, imposing the first ad valorem real estate taxes in 1957 and preparing numerous ordinances and land annexation documents. During his thirty years as city attorney, Miller not only witnessed the city's population grow from fifteen hundred to twelve thousand, but he was also instrumental in creating the legal infrastructure for this to happen. He died in November 2010.

MARCIA STAFFORD

In 1948, Leslie and Marcia Stafford, who lived in Fort Lauderdale, began looking for a place to settle when their first child, son Tracy, was born. They picked Wilton Manors because it had remained dry during the 1947 flood.

They were concerned, however, that the village had no school. Marcia regularly attended Broward School Board meetings, where she was repeatedly assured that "Wilton Manors will never need a school." Knowing what she was going to speak about, they stopped putting her on the agenda, so she would have to wait until the end of the meeting. At this point, she stopped insisting that little Tracy be quiet.

Then she learned Dave Turner had donated land to the municipality on which to build the first school.

Les, Tracy and Marcia Stafford, 1948. *WMHS, Stafford.*

The Staffords headed for the Taylor & Turner Feed Store at Five Points with Tracy in a stroller. Turner sold them a lot for $1,200. When they told him they planned to build on it right away, he lowered the price to $1,000.

Leslie W. Stafford, born in Texas, was the office manager of Eli Witt Cigar and Tobacco Company. Despite a bout with polio, he constructed most of their house himself.

In 1952, Marcia Sawyer Stafford was elected village clerk in a three-way race. She would serve in this capacity for the remainder of the decade, keeping the city's records in her kitchen and conducting much of its business from her home.

The Stafford home at 500 Northeast Twenty-fifth Street became the city's nucleus.

"It was Grand Central Station around here, a steady stream of people," she said. "[There were] policemen, new residents coming in to register and vote. Tracy and Nancy grew up with the business of the city swirling all around them."

Nancy, aged three, went missing one afternoon. Chief Beaney was called and quickly searched all the places she could have gotten to. No trace. When

A modern view of Marcia Stafford's House, built in 1949 with additions. *WMHS, Little.*

he went to report no progress to the now frantic Marcia, he was greeted with "Hi, Chief Beaney!" from a tree in the front yard. Nancy had climbed into a tree for the afternoon.

The city council met in the evening at the village hall (across the street), which was also the meeting place for most of the city's civic organizations.

"You could always tell when the scouts had met there earlier in the day. The place smelled like peanut butter."

Their son Tracy became an attorney and followed his mother into politics. In 1990, he was elected to the Florida House of Representatives, where he served until 2000.

Their daughter, Nancy, a 1975 journalism graduate from the University of Florida, entered the Miss Fort Lauderdale beauty contest, wearing an eight-dollar dress she and her mother bought at a thrift shop. Her hope was to win a scholarship that would send her to graduate school.

She won the Fort Lauderdale contest and went to Orlando for the Miss Florida pageant, this time with a $100 dress. The tall, blue-eyed blonde returned home with the state crown, and with it, a foot in the door of television and commercials. She started out in the soap opera *The Doctors*. She portrayed Joan Halloran in *St. Elsewhere* and moved on to *Matlock*, playing opposite Andy Griffith as Michelle Thomas for six years.

THE VILLAGE OF WILTON MANORS

1947

INC **11** PAGE **96**

First officers of the village of Wilton Manors. *WMHS.*

AFTER THE WAR

Trailer Haven, the first home of many influential Wilton Manors families, circa early 1950s. *WMHS, Lunsford.*

With the end of World War II, the conditions were right for growth, and Wilton Manors' pioneers, Turner, Mickel, Dean, Pedersen, Leaver and Hagen, were well positioned to participate. Like many other farsighted Floridians, they knew it was time for the Sunshine State to grow quickly. Tourists would flock back for vacations in the sun, and many servicemen and women who had trained in Florida would return there to live.

Turner set about selling the 283 lots he had acquired from the Willingham estate in 1945. He began showing young families around Wilton Manors and extolling the advantages of the little community's excellent location. Having acquired them at an average price of forty-four dollars, he could be most generous with his terms.

"I'd give them a deed free and clear to the lots and let them pay me back when they could," he said.

Meanwhile, Al Hagen and Perry Mickel also were selling lots and houses in a Wilton Manors that had expanded far beyond the platted area first introduced by Willingham. Residents came to think of most of the area as Wilton Manors.

With people moving to Florida and building materials still in short supply in the immediate aftermath of World War II, one solution to the housing shortage was to build trailer parks. Wilton Manors had several such parks. Trailer Haven on Wilton Drive near Northeast Ninth Avenue opened in 1947. The Middle River Trailer Park, near Northeast Fifteenth Avenue and Northeast Twenty-fourth Street, had opened by 1949. A trailer park is marked on a 1953 map at the south end of Andrews Avenue, on the west side of the street. It would have been gone by 1955, when Meadowbrook was platted, if it had ever been built. The trailer parks contained not only prefabricated trailers with wheels but also surplus frame army structures and little masonry structures.

Vernon (Vern) Burnell occupied the first trailer at Trailer Haven. He would be elected to the city council in 1956.

Individuals also bought residential lots and built their own homes, often helping one another by bartering their skills. The efforts of Nancy and Bob Sawallis in building their own home on Northwest Twenty-fifth Street in the late 1940s may have been typical.

"SKUNK HOLLOW": THE SAWALLISES

Bob and Nancy Sawallis

As related by Nancy Sawallis to Mary Gayle Ulm in the fall of 2007:

Bob and I came to Fort Lauderdale in 1946. Bob's brother, George, was already in Fort Lauderdale and selling war surplus.

Bob and I bought a platted lot on Northwest Twenty-fifth Street in the subdivision called Beulaland. Northwest Twenty-fifth Street was lined with petticoat palms, and at that time, it

Intersection of Northwest Twenty-fifth Street and Northwest Third Avenue, circa 1946. *WMHS, Sawallis.*

was only a block long, running to the start of the Mickel property, where Northwest Third Avenue is today.

Our lot bordered the Mickel property to the west and the Coggin property to the east (now apartments). Besides the Mickels, Coggins and our house, there was only one other house on Northwest Twenty-fifth Street: the Clark House still at 124 Northwest Twenty-fifth Street.

Bob built our first house by hand. Perry Mickel and his two sons, John and Bob, helped Bob lay the foundation. We built our house on the back portion of our lot because we planned on building a larger structure for ourselves closer to Northwest Twenty-fifth Street, once we were better established in the community and could afford something larger.

Our house was simple but quite comfortable. Across its front we built a sleeping porch that had jalousie windows on three sides of the structure. We had a small kitchen and bathroom and a large closet with built-in drawers.

We called our house Skunk Hollow because one night we awoke to the sound of pots and pans rattling in our kitchen. A skunk had gotten in through a portion of the house that was not completed.

The Mickels were very dear to Bob and me and made wonderful neighbors. They shared the culls of the vegetables they raised, such as corn and green beans, which were taken to market

Sawallis home, called Skunk Hollow, under construction, circa 1945. *WMHS, Sawallis.*

> *in Pompano. They had chickens and cows and at least one horse. One of the Mickel children was knocked off the horse because they ran into my clothesline.*
>
> *One of the first homes built by Perry when he subdivided his property was a duplex at the corner of Twenty-fifth Street and Third Avenue. The Mickels' caretaker's shack, occupied by an African American gentleman named Willie, was located where the duplex currently sits.*
>
> *Gordon A. Gilbertson and his wife moved into the duplex. We enjoyed having the Gilbertsons as neighbors very much.*

GROWING A COMMUNITY

By the spring of 1946, the adult population of Wilton Manors had grown to about 125. On May 10, a group of homeowners met at the office of Al Hagen to form the first Wilton Manors Civic Association. The group elected A.O. Lefler as its chairman, James A. Boyd as vice-chairman and Katherine Johnson as secretary/treasurer. Several committees were formed: transportation, headed by Dave Turner and A.F. Camman; street improvements, headed by James Farquhar and Harley Sanderson; and water, headed by John Pedersen and Al Hagen. (By 1957, the Civic Association had outlived its usefulness, and its assets were transferred to the budding library project. It was revived in 1981 by a group of citizens and lasted until 2006.)

Members set out to improve water, garbage pickup and electrical service to the area; the transportation committee worked to bring better bus service and improved street maintenance. Speeding on Wilton Drive was a problem, and requests were made to the county commission and Sheriff Walter Clark to enforce the speed limits. This has been a perennial problem.

At the November 1 meeting, the members discussed ways to prevent annexation by Fort Lauderdale. Jim Boyd's minutes from the meeting reflect the suggestions of a new member, Colonel William J. Robinson, an attorney: "Mr. Robinson pointed out that the City of Fort Lauderdale was heavily indebted from the boom-bust of 1927, and if the city were to take this area in we would be paying these taxes, while if we incorporated into a village any taxes assessed the village would get the benefit, and these would only be levied by the will of the people."

Wilton Manors pushed for incorporation. On December 6, the Civic Association passed a motion requesting that Robinson draft a petition for incorporation. By the first meeting of 1947, the incorporation drive had moved ahead so far and so quickly that the Highland Estates Association, representing homeowners in that subdivision, sent three representatives to the meeting. The Highland Estates subdivision is east of Northeast Sixth Avenue between Northeast Twenty-sixth Street and the North Fork of the Middle River. There were many homes there that were "works in progress," their owners working on them in the winter and returning north in the summers, leaving them unfinished. The Highland Estates group was concerned that building codes and restrictions would be stricter than it wanted.

The next month, a preliminary petition circulated in the community and gave the Civic Association an official picture of how sentiments were running. Eighty-seven favored and ten opposed incorporation. The association needed twenty-five more registered voters to make its petition official. Meanwhile, Highland Estates decided against joining with Wilton Manors.

"THE BIG MEETING"

At the April 4 meeting, the Civic Association scheduled what its minutes called the "Big Meeting." The notice said that it was to be held at the Tropical Homes offices, either inside or out, at 8:00 p.m. on April 28. Al Hagen opened the meeting and turned it over to Colonel Robinson. While the perennial threat had been Fort Lauderdale, both Hagen and Robinson mentioned an imminent threat of annexation from Oakland Park. Discussion was lively. Highland Estates and Lazy Lake had opted out prior to the meeting. John Pedersen, one of the largest landholders in the Fort Lauderdale area, seems to have been opposed. Nevertheless, the motion passed, and Colonel Robinson was authorized to take the legal steps to convert the petitions into official status as the village of Wilton Manors. A mayor and aldermen were elected.

The Village of Wilton Manors was to have an eastern border of the FEC tracks, from the South Fork of the Middle River to Prospect Road (Northeast Twenty-sixth Street). The western border was a line twelve hundred feet west of Andrews Avenue (what is now Northwest Fifth Avenue) from Northeast Twenty-sixth Street to the South Fork of the Middle River. The northern border was Northeast Twenty-sixth Street from the FEC tracks to the line west of Andrews Avenue. The southern border was the South Fork of the Middle River from this line west of Andrews to the FEC railroad tracks.

The Village of Wilton Manors

Conspicuously excluded from the village were the Richardson Golf Course (now Richardson Park and the Manor Grove condominiums, from Wilton Drive to Andrews Avenue along the river) and Lazy Lake, a subdivision bounded by Andrews Avenue, Northeast Twenty-first Court, Northeast First Avenue and Northeast Twenty-fourth Street.

On April 28, 1947, the Broward County Circuit Court accepted Robinson's petition, declaring that what had started as a small subdivision in 1926 now qualified as a municipal corporation to be known as the Village of Wilton Manors, with a population of roughly 350. The slate elected at the April 28 meeting became the village's first officers. Curiously, the aldermen were now councilmen. Turner was mayor and municipal judge. Alvar Hagen was president of the village council, serving with Arthur Chabot; Colonel Robinson, who doubled as the village's first attorney; James Boyd; and J. Marvin Brown. Katherine V. Johnson became the village clerk. Boyd and Brown were elected to three-year terms. The others were all reelected in the second village election on November 8, 1949, and Boyd and Brown were reelected unopposed on November 11, 1950.

The first town meetings were held in Hagen's real estate offices on Wilton Drive. From 1947 to 1952, Wilton Manors records were stored in Colonel Robinson's law offices.

On May 13, 1947, the State of Florida completed its processing of the paperwork sent to Tallahassee and declared the community officially the Village of Wilton Manors, legally separated from Fort Lauderdale. There were no property taxes. Revenue was received from fees on occupational, beverage and power franchise licenses and from a cigarette tax. Village barbecues were held to fund special projects.

Village barbecue. Upside-down fruit baskets were used as both tables and chairs, circa 1948. *WMHS, Woman's Club.*

Now that Wilton Manors was a separate entity, its elected officials and civic organizations needed a place to meet. Accordingly, Dave Turner donated a piece of land on the southeast corner of Northeast Twenty-sixth Street and Northeast Fifth Avenue, and volunteers built a small meeting hall.

THE NEW VILLAGE

In 1947, the population of Broward County was fewer than eighty thousand. Television sets were just beginning to appear in private homes in 1947, the year President Harry S Truman dedicated Everglades National Park.

Willingham's towers still stood guard at the north end of Wilton Drive. Gwen Mace was born on Mother's Day 1947 and came from the hospital to her parents' new home, the southeast tower. Her grandfather, Merle D. Mace, owned much of the Point, defined by Wilton Drive and Dixie Highway. His home was where the Kalis Funeral Home is now. They added a two-story addition to the back of the largest tower. Gwen Mace, now King, remembers goats wandering in the fields east of Five Points.

On September 16, 1948, the *Broward Sun* reported that Governor-elect Fuller Warren, in the presence of Mayor Dave Turner, attacked the Florida legislature "for refusing to protect residents of the state from the menace of roaming livestock on the highways."

The rainy season came early in 1947. The wet spring was followed by an even wetter summer. In the fall, within twenty-five days, two hurricanes and a tropical disturbance dropped so much rain on the area that much of southeastern Florida lay under water for weeks. Fort Lauderdale and Pompano Beach were flooded, and Davie was covered with an inland sea for months. Most of Wilton Manors remained convincingly above water.

The rains gave real estate developers in Wilton Manors another powerful marketing tool, adding "high and dry" to "convenient location" and the ever-enticing "no city taxes."

The flooding was so severe that the Central and Southern Florida Flood Control District was created to try to prevent future floods. The first chairman of the flood control district was Wilton Manors mayor Dave Turner.

After the storms, Alvar Hagen measured the high-water mark at the Northeast Fourth Avenue bridge. He undertook the dredging of the southeast fork of the Middle River and filled land to a point one foot higher than the high-water mark, which later enabled the building of residential communities along the river there.

The Village of Wilton Manors

A sign touting Wilton Manors on Wilton Drive, circa 1947. *WMHS.*

Wilton Manors worked hard to keep its budget lean. None of the elected officials was paid, and no costs were incurred for maintaining a village hall. In the early days, the main expenses were street maintenance and a small volunteer fire department. Harley Sanderson was the town marshal. In August 1947, Broward sheriff Walter Clark appointed Paul Mack as a deputy to Sanderson to help police the town. Sanderson retired in 1949 and was replaced by Mark Mitchell Jr.

Not everyone was happy with Wilton Manors. The *Broward Sun* reported on October 21, 1948, that John Pedersen "and others" had filed a petition to be excluded from the village of Wilton Manors. No specific reason was provided. The village set out to determine who was thinking this was a good idea. Did they own their lots or were they leasing from Pedersen? The village also wanted to know the feelings in general of the people who lived in the area. The village council backed this up by authorizing funds to defend the village. It appears that the move on the part of Pedersen was abandoned.[27]

The November 21, 1948 *Broward Sunday Sun*'s House and Home section featured Wilton Manors: "To reach this suburban community, situated well above high water, you drive out Andrews Avenue, cross the railroad tracks and parallel them to northeast Fourth Avenue. Drive north on this street until you cross a bridge, which is over the north [should be south] fork of the Middle River."[28] Residents frequently referred to Wilton Manors as "out here," quite distinct from anything to the south.

The residents were described as "mostly retired, or semi-retired business men from all over the country who have built substantial homes there, and take an interest in its growth."[29]

> *It is free of city taxes, but has a stringent building code.*
>
> *The shopping center boasts a large super-market, and a modern self-service laundry.*
>
> *Bordering Wilton Manors on the south, is the Richardson Golf Course, a sporty nine-holes, very popular with those who find the Country Club crowded…*
>
> *Much of the property is owned and has been developed by the Tropical Homes Company, in which Clayton Leavor* [sic] *and A. Hagan* [sic] *are associates.*[30]

In November 1949, the village got electric streetlights.

In the 1950s, residents bought cards and gifts from Mr. and Mrs. McGilligan's shop, just south of Manor Market. Mr. McGilligan was blind, but when new cards came in, his wife would read him the verses. When a customer went into the shop and told him what he was looking for, Mr. McGilligan would pick exactly the right card from the display.

Rothe's Garage, which had replaced the Atlantic gas station at the corner of Northeast Twenty-first Court and Wilton Drive, was the place to get cars fixed. People came from as far away as Palm Beach.

LIFE IN THE NEW VILLAGE

Dave Turner gave Lamar Braddy land on the 2200 block of Wilton Drive at Sixth Avenue in 1946 to open a market. The arrangement, which seems typical of Turner, was that once the market got on its feet, he would be repaid for the land. Braddy brought on the much younger Frank Starling and made him a full partner without any cash investment.

Starling handled the day-to-day operation of the store and product marketing. Braddy drove to the Homestead Farmer's Market to hand select the day's fresh produce. Initially, the store had dirt floors and was partially

open to the elements. It was staffed
by Starling, his wife Mary, Braddy
and two butchers. The store was
an immediate success and became
the social hub of the community
and the site of the community's
first public telephone. In time, it is
reported to have employed nearly
sixty people.

Manor Market specialized in
prime beef. Braddy purchased
a steer and kept it outside the
market as a promotion of its
future offering for butcher and
sale. There are newspaper articles
about importing 100,000 pounds
of beef, four carloads full, from
New Zealand to be sold at the store. The publicity value is priceless. The
logistics suggest some hyperbole. The beef was frozen. The family did not
partake, as they did not eat meat that had been frozen.[31]

Lamar Braddy, circa 1950s. *WMHS, Eakin.*

When money was needed to build the baseball field on land leased to the
city by Perry Mickel, Braddy purchased a boat and sold raffle tickets at the
store. Braddy's son won the raffle because Braddy purchased the majority of
the tickets. For years, the baseball diamond at the field was named for Braddy.

In 1952, Braddy and Starling undertook a reported $75,000 expansion of
Manor Market, which included a two-acre parking lot in the rear. There were
disputes with the neighbors over a zoning variance. In November 1952, Braddy
and Starling celebrated the renovation with a three-day sale, which drew a
reported twenty thousand people. The staff could hardly keep up with the crush.

Manor Market, circa 1949. *WMHS/BCHC.*

"Catfish Annie," who lived in a cardboard piano box on Sunrise Boulevard, would periodically stop by Manor Market. Mr. Braddy had left orders with the butcher to give her a free chicken. One day, Annie complained that the chickens that the butcher was giving her were "puny." Mr. Braddy then instructed the butcher that she was to receive nice-sized ones.

One of Wilton Manors' wealthier residents frequently managed to get out of Manors Market without paying for everything. Mr. Braddy had a quiet word with the customer's husband, who admitted to the ongoing problem and reimbursed the store after such shopping trips.

Before coming to Wilton Manors, Braddy owned Southside Market and had interests in Bass Brother's Market, Fifth Avenue Market and a casino called Club Greyhound, with ties to infamous Sherriff Walter C. Clark. He and Starling embarked on a number of other business ventures, including a muffler shop and the Flame Restaurant.

Braddy was generous, enthusiastic and outgoing. He also gambled. The importance of Braddy's Manor Market as a focus of social activity in early Wilton Manors cannot be overemphasized. Braddy died an untimely death in 1959 and left a complicated estate. His daughter reports that there was a box of "IOUs" worth thousands of dollars for credit extended to Manor Market customers. Braddy was a kind and good neighbor.

Food Fair grand opening, *Fort Lauderdale News*, February 14, 1953. *WMHS.*

In July 1952, Food Fair, Inc., bought property at 2020 Wilton Drive, Alvar Hagen's golf driving range on the east side of the street, and announced plans to build the town's first chain supermarket, "one of the most modern stores of its kind in this area" and "completely air-conditioned."[32] It opened in February 1953.

There was no shortage of places to buy food. Manor Market was the first "big deal." Chain stores followed as formidable competition. About 1954, a Kwik Chek (later Winn-Dixie) was built at Sunrise and Powerline and was a handy favorite for those on the west side of town. Later came Stevens Market (at the current Shoppes at Wilton Manors). The original Food Fair was expanded and became Frederichs Supermarket, and an A&P opened in Manor Gate Center (where the Old Florida Seafood Restaurant is now). Frederichs Supermarket had an unfortunate distinction. The "F" dropped off the sign one day and killed a man. In 1959, Publix purchased the Grand Union food store that had opened in the Five Points Plaza in the mid-1950s. A bit later, Kwik Chek built its first Wilton Manors store at the corner of Northwest Twenty-ninth Street and Andrews Avenue. It became a Winn-Dixie and then a Walgreens. Readers with an archaeological interest will, as of this writing, find a sign in the parking lot restricting parking to Winn-Dixie shoppers only. Stevens Market became a Grand Union food store and then a Piggly Wiggly, which closed in 1988.

A chicken farm on Oakland Park Boulevard, just east of Northeast Sixth Avenue and the current Kmart, sold fresh eggs; cracked eggs were sold at a significant discount. Fresh hens, dressed or not, were also available.

By 1958, Braddy and Starling had sold Manor Market and opened an auto muffler and tailpipe installation business at 2223 Wilton Drive. After an argument over the business and Braddy's untimely death in 1959, Starling became a partner in the Manor Flame restaurant, later named The Palms. This then became Chardee's, the city's first restaurant to cater to a gay clientele. Today, the structure still stands as part of the Plaza Dee North strip shopping center on Wilton Drive adjacent to Northeast Sixth Avenue.

In the 1930s and during the war, money was tight, and people preferred to entertain at home. A meal out was something at the drugstore lunch counter. Bob and Nancy Sawallis had a pressure cooker and a hot plate in their one-room apartment.

By the 1940s, purse strings had loosened a bit. Neighbors organized square dances at one of their houses or a potluck dinner on the beach. A drive up Dixie Highway on a Sunday was entertainment.

A trip to the movies required a journey to Fort Lauderdale to visit the Florida, the Warner, the Colony or the State, which were one-screen theaters. There was a drive-in movie theater on Andrews Avenue in Oakland

Wilton Manors Bulletin, July 19, 1951. *WMHS.*

Park called the North Andrews Gardens Drive-In.

In May 1952, the Tropical Club Patio on Wilton Drive advertised Monday, Thursday and Saturday dinner specials for ninety-five cents. The Sunday special was $1.75 for the prime rib or $1.45 for the leg of lamb. Fort Lauderdale offered a number of restaurants popular with Wilton Manors residents. Reliable and inexpensive places included the Blue Plate Special in Fort Lauderdale, the Sea Grill on Northeast Fourth Avenue (across the street from the high school), Tail of the Tiger, Charcoal Smokehouse, Diney's Drive In (with car hops), Johnnie's El Dorado (Italian) and Dumars' Drive In, with flying saucers as part of the décor. The Dairy Queen, on Wilton Drive since 1953, and Brown's, on Andrews Avenue at Northwest Twenty-ninth Street, served family fare.

Irwin "Red" Barnwell opened Red's Bar & Package Store in 1949. His wife, Rosella, was the bookkeeper. They purchased a property just north of Five Points on Dixie Highway and moved an old barracks building, purchased for $650, from the Boca Raton Army Airfield to the site. The building had survived the two 1947 hurricanes and remains today one of Wilton Manors' important landmarks and watering holes. Rosella's father built the bar's interior, and the two men later added the adjoining package store. Air conditioning arrived in 1964. Rosella Barnwell died in 1970; Red Barnwell died in 1972.

Chickens were still permitted in Wilton Manors in the 1950s. Every morning, Rachel Richardson would take a small basket of eggs across the street to her neighbor, Ginny Hagen.

As far as is known, Wilton Manors could boast only one bomb shelter. When the house on Northeast Fifth Avenue and Northeast Twenty-fifth Street was torn down to make room for the expanded library in 2001, it was nearly impervious to the wrecking ball.

Wilton Manors was home to at least one house of ill repute. At one point, it was known as the Sporting Inn. Reliable sources are embarrassed to confirm that, over time, there were two others on Northeast Twenty-sixth Street and a third at the east end of town.

The front page of the *Wilton Manors Bulletin* on Thursday, January 8, 1953, captures the spirit of the time. "Newsy Notes" listed residents' activities, such as who had gone on vacation, who had returned and who was visiting. This was small-town life: The annual election of officers of the Highland Estates Civic Club was held. Santa brought a horse to Gary Swinea, twelve. There was some sports news, weather news designed to attract tourists and kudos to the people who arranged the Christmas display downtown. Business leaders predicted a big year for the area. Jerry Kessel, age about four years, broke his collarbone, and seventy-six bicycle owners got license tags for their bicycles, at seventy-five cents each.

A pamphlet published by the Wilton Manors Historical Society enumerates the changes between 1950 and 1955. In 1950, there were eighteen businesses on Wilton Drive. In 1955, six of these were still operating, joined by another eighty citywide. In 1950, there were 250 homes. By 1955, there were 1,500. The city was approximately one square mile. By 1955, it had doubled in size. In 1955, about five thousand lots were still available, and a population of fifteen thousand was thought to be easily attainable. The city employed twelve people.

CIVIC AND SOCIAL ORGANIZATIONS

By the end of 1949, the population had grown to seven hundred. A village meeting hall had been built at 500 Northeast Twenty-sixth Street under the guidance of Clayton Leaver on land donated by Dave Turner. In time, residents would need more elaborate city services. In the November 8, 1949 election, they voted seventy-four to four against the question: "Are you in favor of levying ad valorem taxes against real estate?"

On February 22, 1950, Floyd Miller was hired as a police officer to protect the town's 250 homes and 883 residents. Sheriff Clark gave him a two-way radio, and Wilton Manors provided him with a police car.

The Wilton Manors Civic Association was started in 1946 and had been the catalyst for the founding of the village. The Highland Estates Civic Association, founded prior to 1947, was the de facto government in Highland Estates. By 1955, civic and social organizations had grown to include the Kiwanis Club, Sinawiks, the Wilton Manors Business Group, the Jaycees and Jaycee-ettes, the Junior Woman's Club, the Lions Club, Little League Baseball and Wilton Manors Sports, Inc. A chapter of the Parent-Teachers Association was formed to support the Wilton Manors Elementary School, which had opened before the end of the 1951–52 school year with 183 students.

The Woman's Club of Wilton Manors started in 1948 at an organizational meeting in the Tropical Club on Wilton Drive. It was recognized by the National Federation of Woman's Clubs on April 5, 1949, and grew from thirty-two members in that year to eighty-five in 1962. It originally met in the village meeting hall on Northeast Twenty-sixth Street. Ground for the permanent clubhouse at 600 Northeast Twenty-first Court was broken in April 1955 on land donated by Alvar and Virginia Hagen.

Woman's Club, built in 1955. *WMHS, Woman's Club.*

For almost sixty years, members of the Woman's Club have contributed to the civic, cultural, educational and social life of the city. They have supported innumerable philanthropic causes, and they have maintained their clubhouse solely through private means. In July 2007, the city commission granted historic landmark status to the building.

The Civic Association's announcement of the Christmas Committee in November 20, 1952, is instructive in understanding the role of women in the 1950s. James Dean, Earle Middleton, Robert Newman, A. Saxer and Guy Smith were appointed to the committee. Mrs. Dave Turner, Mrs. Robert Newton, Mrs. Alvar Hagen, Mrs. T.A. Miller and Mrs. Gordon Sanderson, among others, were named to an advisory committee.[33]

BRICK AND MORTAR GROWTH

New businesses continued to move in. A Dairy Queen opened in 1953 at the south end of Wilton Drive, and after several modernizations, it is still there. Kalis Funeral Home opened in 1959 at Five Points, at the same time Publix took over the Grand Union just to the north.

The *Wilton Oakland Sun* of August 13, 1953, reported, "Pool Is Badly Needed, City Fathers Admit." Mayor Mickel supported the idea. Chief Beaney thought it was a great idea, pointing "to continuous difficulties with youngsters who have nothing to occupy their minds and energies."[34] It was tentatively to be funded by a revenue bond. Where to put it and funding

Publix supermarket grand opening, 1965. *WMHS, Publix supermarkets.*

Volunteer Fire Department, with VFD 2, circa 1952. *WMHS.*

were listed as problems to be worked out. It was never built. As part of the Jenada Villas development, a pool was built on Northwest Twenty-ninth Street in the 1950s. It is now the site of Donn Eisele Park.

In 1952, village council president Charles A. Saxer announced the formation of the forty-two-member Wilton Manors Volunteer Fire Department. Saxer had retired after thirty years with the U.S. Steel Corporation in New York and had moved to Wilton Manors in 1950. Among the early volunteers were Police Chief Beaney, historian and author Norman Malcolm, councilman Frank Starling, Fred Haberstitch and Al Walker, who also served as chief. The core of the 1952 department was the Highland Estates Volunteer Fire Department, inherited as part of the annexation of Highland Estates. It was housed in the east end of the city hall on Northeast Twenty-first Court and got its own, purpose-built station on Northeast Twenty-second Street in 1969.

Recreation programs were put together by volunteers. Al Hagen donated his old golf driving range on Wilton Drive for a park. In 1955, a shuffleboard court was installed.

That spring, Mayor Perry Mickel granted Wilton Manors Sports, Inc., a five-year lease at a dollar a year for a ball field located just east of Powerline Road to create a Little League Baseball facility. The city bought the property for $21,000 from Mickel and named it Mickel Field in 1960.

ELEMENTARY SCHOOL

As early as the 1920s, there were schools in the area. Mark Mahannah remembers going to school for part of one year in Oakland Park, but most of the children in Colohatchee, Oakland Park and Wilton Manors attended school in Fort Lauderdale. Children from this area went to Northside Elementary at 120 Northeast Eleventh Street until fifth or sixth grade. All then went to Central High at 1600 Northeast Fourth Avenue.

Remarkably, several people interviewed for this book not only remembered their classmates' names from the 1920s and 1930s but also exactly where they lived. Broward County provided bus service, so all the children knew one another. "Bus service" from Colohatchee in the early days was a horse-drawn cart.

On April 2, 1951, ground was broken for the Wilton Manors Elementary School on Northeast Twenty-fourth Street, built on land that had been covered with slash pines, palmettos and wild cactus. It occupied four square blocks, from Northeast Third Avenue to Northeast Fifth Avenue and from Northeast Twenty-fourth Street to Northeast Twenty-sixth Street. One of Pedersen's chicken farms was located on the other side of Northeast Twenty-third Street. More exciting were the neighbors across Northeast Twenty-fourth Street at Northeast Third Avenue: the former Sporting Inn, allegedly a brothel. Construction workers on the school kept finding empty whiskey bottles where the proprietors of the Sporting Inn, trying to keep a low profile, had buried them. James Dean reports that he insured the building, which was later converted into a nursing home.

Before 1951 was out, the school, headed by its first principal, W. Bryan Davis, was ready for 183 students. Within a year, enrollment had grown to 310, and the school was seriously overcrowded. In September 1952, the County Disaster Relief Committee designated the school a hurricane shelter. By 2008, enrollment had grown to over 600 students, and the rebuilt and much larger school now faces Northeast Twenty-sixth Street. As of 2009, Wilton Manors Elementary is the only school in Broward County

Wilton Manors
Elementary School,
circa 1952. *WMES.*

that participates in the International Baccalaureate Organization's Primary Years Programme. This program draws on research and the best practices from several national and international school systems. The school has been the recipient of numerous local, state and national awards and grants.

1952 VILLAGE COUNCIL AND PUBLIC SAFETY

In 1952, Dave Turner stepped down as mayor, and Perry Mickel was elected to replace him on March 3. Joining him on the council were J. Frank Starling, who would succeed him three years later; Earle Middleton, who became council president; and James Dean. They joined sitting council members James Boyd and J. Marvin Brown. Marcia Stafford was elected village clerk.

At its organizational meeting on March 11, the new council hired William G. Miller Jr., a 1950 law school graduate, as village counsel at a monthly fee of ten dollars, succeeding Colonel Robinson. Miller's father had been Broward County's prosecutor from 1932 to 1947. Miller would hold the position, renamed city attorney, for the next thirty years.

Mickel authorized creation of a police department. Richard Beaney was hired as chief for $70 a week. Robert S. Hickman was hired as patrol officer. In November 1952, Beaney convinced the mayor and council that another patrol officer was needed, so James Carrie was hired. The department also bought a 1950 Harley Davidson motorcycle for $450.

Wilton Manors "liked Ike" a lot, giving Dwight D. Eisenhower a 779 to 258 edge over Democrat Adlai Stevenson in the 1952 presidential election.

By 1952, the lack of a water infrastructure could not be ignored. Expansion of the community depended on a reliable and affordable water distribution system. The question was whether to buy water from Oakland Park or Fort Lauderdale or develop a local water treatment facility. After much discussion, including negotiation with Highland Estates over its water distribution system, Wilton Manors signed an agreement with Oakland Park.[35]

In an ordinance approved on September 9, 1952, the village council established a Water Department to handle the distribution of water and collection of water revenues. The department was headed by city engineer O.M. Dunton, with Wally Wakely as water superintendent. The cost to business and residential customers to have a water meter installed was set at $50.00 per meter. Water was billed at $2.50 per month for up to five thousand gallons. Water bills could be paid at the temporary Water Department office, located in Frank Miller's Hardware Store at 2114 Wilton Drive.

THE CITY OF
WILTON MANORS
1953

WILTON ☀ SUN OAKLAND

Volume 1 — Number 25   Thursday, February 26, 1953

GRAB WILTON MANORS? NOT TODAY, COUNCIL VOWS

Our Own Homogenized

Hot Air

By CARTER HOLMES

It appears that the entire political structure of Wilton Manors may be altered by the revelation that Fort Lauderdale would like to reach out and take Wilton Manors and Oakland Park into its sandpile for its hungry little politicians to dig into. And Oakland Park may very well follow with some action of its own when its Council meets next week.

And it may mean, dear friends, that a little taxation for Village property owners is just around the corner. But don't get unduly excited, because that might not be so bad, at that.

It other words, 7 mills, say, would be better than, say, 17.

NOW EVERYBODY KNOWS FOR WHOM SIREN BLOWS

Ever wonder who toots the Wilton Manors siren every evening at 6 o'clock?

It's Eleanor Christensen, who operates a dry cleaning shop at Market where the siren control button is installed.

About a year and a half ago, there were two occasions when firemen weren't called to a fire because the thing refused to

Council Moves Swiftly To Stall Any Effort Toward Annexing Community

Wilton Manors Village Council took serious note this week of reports published in The Sun that Ft. Lauderdale has fastened hungry eyes on this community. And the result was fast action to let anybody concerned know there's nothing doing if Council can help it. Or, as grandpaw used to say whe the kids asked for a quarter: "There ain't a pea on the vine."

The subject was first brought up by Councilman J. Marvin Brown who directed at Village Attorney Bill Miller the question:

"What chance has Ft. Lauder-

School Children "Hep" When It Comes To Flag

Norman Malcolm, 2310 NE Fifth Ave., is thoroughly satisfied with

Wilton Oakland Sun, November 12, 1953. WMHS.

THWARTING A LAND GRAB

The *Wilton Oakland Sun*, in a full-page headline on February 26, 1953, proclaimed "Grab Wilton Manors? Not Today, Council Vows." Columnist Carter Holmes wrote, "It appears that the entire political structure of Wilton Manors may be altered by the revelation that Fort Lauderdale would like to reach out and take Wilton Manors and Oakland Park into its sand pile for its hungry little politicians to dig into."[36] It was time to move up from village to city.

"We really incorporated to prevent a takeover by Fort Lauderdale," explained city attorney William Miller.

As a village, Wilton Manors was a nonprofit organization, approved routinely by the Broward County Circuit Court. Becoming a city offered more potential for self-rule and an improved financial standing. To become a city, Wilton Manors required the approval of the state legislature.

James Dean, village council president, and William Miller personally carried the Articles of Incorporation that Miller had drafted to Tallahassee. On June 4, 1953, Wilton Manors officially became the eleventh city in Broward County.

A day earlier, to prevent a takeover by Wilton Manors, the village of Lazy Lake, with fewer than thirty residents, became incorporated. Charles Lindfors was named the first mayor and served for eight terms until his death in August 1969.

THE COUNCIL DIVIDED

The city of Wilton Manors in 1953 was a far cry from Willingham's plat. Hagen, Mickel, Dean and others had been busily developing the areas beyond the original core, expanding west of Andrews Avenue, east of the Florida East Coast Railway tracks and north of Northeast Twenty-sixth Street.

The election of November 1953 demonstrated, however, that not all the early city leaders were marching to the same drummer. "New Wilton Manors Council Split Wide Open" was the five-column headline in the *Wilton Oakland Sun* after the first city council meeting following the November 10, 1953 election.

Mayor Perry Mickel and city clerk Marcia Stafford were reelected without opposition.

Of the 305 ballots cast in the city council race, incumbent Frank Starling received 154 votes. Clarence B. Riggs received 134, and Charles A. Saxer, 118, making them the two new faces on the council. Retiring council

The City of Wilton Manors

New Wilton Manors Council Split Wide Open

EDITORIAL COMMENT—

Good Turnout, Bad Politics

By Carter Holmes

The people have spoken. Or, rather, half of the people have spoken.

Only 305 ballots were cast out of more than 600 registered voters in last week's election.

At that, it was a pretty fair turnout, just 63 less than voted last year when the Presidential election brought them to the polls.

It appeared for a time we would have a reasonably clean election. Then, only some three or four days before election day, someone started circulating a rumor to the effect that the deed to the city hall site east of the FEC, given to the city by

Oakland Park Race Gets 3 Candidates

Three candidates were entered this week in Oakland Park's 1953 city political contests for mayor, city clerk and city council.

Councilman Charles M. Hunter qualified as a candidate for re-election while W. Ralph Green, president of the Oakland Park Volunteer Fire Department, also became a contender for one of the three city council vacancies.

Gurney Gets Council Presidency On 2-2 Vote Under Rules of Procedure

A new Wilton Manors City Council was "organized" Tuesday night. It took less than 2 minutes for it to become the most disorganized ever seen in the Village Hall. The Council, with two new faces at the table, promptly split wide open and evidently will stay that way for an indefinite time. The two new faces were those of Clarence B. Riggs and Charles A. Saxer, who were elected over Earle L. Middleton and James C. Dean last week.

The third candidate elected was Starling who led the entire field by a wide margin with 154 votes out of 305 ballots cast in the elec-

Starling & Brown On Outside Looking In

The five members of the new Wilton Manors City Council met for an informal lunch

Wilton Oakland Sun, November 12, 1953. *WMHS.*

president and incumbent Earle L. Middleton lost with 117. James Dean was also defeated, with 108 votes.

The article began, "A new Wilton Manors City Council was 'organized' Tuesday night. It took less than two minutes for it to become the most disorganized ever seen in the Village Hall."[37]

A new city hall was in the works, and Dean and Turner had offered to give land to the city on which to build it. The land was east of the FEC tracks and part of their proposed huge shopping and office complex: Manor Gate.

Just prior to the election, ugly rumors circulated that the gift of a deed came with unpublished trick clauses. All five members of the new council met for lunch on Monday, the day before the first council meeting, apparently to bury some hatchets. Neither Starling nor incumbent J. Marvin Brown was invited to a later meeting at 11:00 a.m. on Tuesday at incumbent Earl Gurney's house.

At the Tuesday night council meeting, Saxer nominated Gurney for council president, seconded by Riggs. Brown nominated Starling on the grounds that he was the highest vote-getter in the election. Starling nominated Brown on the grounds that he had the most experience on the council.

Stalemate.

The city attorney, William G. Miller, ruled that Earl Gurney would be president, as his was the only nomination that had been seconded.

Much parliamentary maneuvering resulted in no one being appointed police commissioner or road commissioner. The article in the *Wilton Oakland Sun* ended: "It looked like a long winter might be ahead."[38]

Wilton Manors National Bank, circa 1958. *WMHS, Crabtree.*

Their second meeting, on December 8, failed to achieve a compromise on police commissioner. The city charter allowed for the mayor to take over the appointment. Starling moved to do so, seconded by Riggs.

The controversy about the new city hall continued on for another three years.

In the November 1954 election, Marcia Stafford was elected to her third term as city clerk. George Richardson Jr., at age thirty-five, was elected to his first term, and Earle Middleton returned for his second term, having been voted off the previous year.

On April 28, 1955, the Wilton Manors National Bank opened at Northeast Twenty-sixth Street and Fifteenth Avenue. The founder was Clay D. Dyal Jr., son of an Orlando banker. He most probably had the support and encouragement of the local luminaries who were named "charter directors," including Dean, Middleton, Turner and Fred Williams. The building was designed by Charles McKirahan, one of the fathers of Mid-Century Modern architecture. Until recently, it was a branch of SunTrust Banks, Inc.

Vern Burnell (city council member from 1956 to 1960) stated in a 1975 interview with the historical society that he disagreed with the location for the bank on Northeast Twenty-sixth Street because it necessitated curving Northeast Fifteenth Avenue to the east as it approached Northeast Twenty-sixth Street from the south, where it joins Northeast Sixteenth Avenue, adding to the frustrations of Wilton Manors residents and visitors who expect a solid "grid" with street names.

Northeast Fifteenth/Sixteenth Avenue was a logical north–south corridor. A Northeast Sixteenth Avenue bridge across the North Fork of the Middle River into Oakland Park was thwarted by developers who owned land on the North Fork. Burnell went to the county and convinced it to transfer the funds to build a bridge at Northeast Sixth Avenue. Mr. M.C. Slagle donated twenty-five feet from his land to create the necessary width in the last block before the bridge. Wilton Manors contributed $5,000 for the construction of the bridge, and the county contributed $35,000 and paved Northeast Sixth Avenue for the first time.

In the 1960s, Broward County declared Northeast Sixteenth Avenue a county road, which allowed construction of the bridge that had previously been opposed.

CHURCHES

Willingham was a deacon in the Baptist Church, and religious worship has been important to Wilton Manors residents from the beginning.

The Covenant Presbyterian Church was organized by Ann Wilmarth in January 1949 with thirty-three charter members under the sponsorship of the Bethany Presbyterian Church in Fort Lauderdale. The church's first services were held in the Highland Estates Civic Association building on Northeast Eighth Avenue. Reverend Russell Toms became the church's first full-time pastor. Dave Turner donated the land where the church built its first chapel in 1949 at 512 Northeast Twenty-sixth Street, its current location.

The Wilton Manors Baptist Chapel was organized as a mission of the First Baptist Church of Fort Lauderdale, and Reverend A.D. Dawson was appointed as pastor. Services were first held in the home of Robert and Grace Newton, who moved to Wilton Manors in 1947. The Baptist congregation held its first large, formal service in December 1953 in the Willingham Gatehouse Tower. In January 1954, ground was broken for construction of a church at 116 Northeast Twenty-fourth Street, near the elementary school. Reverend Kelly Blanton became pastor in August 1954, and the Wilton Manors Baptist Church was formally established on July 10, 1955, with 151 members, including James Dean. A two-story educational building opened in 1958. The current church building, with a seating capacity of 400, was dedicated on July 25, 1970.

In May 1952, the Roman Catholic Archdiocese in Florida purchased twelve acres of land at the corner of North Andrews Avenue and Northwest Twenty-ninth Street. Father James Keogh was sent by Bishop Joseph Hurley, Diocese of St. Augustine, to organize the Catholic community in the area. The St. Clement Church Hall was dedicated in December 1955, and religious services were held there until the current church at 2975 North Andrews was completed in 1970.

A two-story school building was built in 1956 behind the church hall, followed by a convent and rectory in 1961. Father Keogh remained pastor until 1963. In 2009, the school reopened as Somerset Academy Charter School.

The First Christian Church of Wilton Manors, located at 2725 Northeast Fourteenth Avenue, opened its doors on April 10, 1955. Its founding pastor was Reverend Clarence Stauffer, who was succeeded by his son, Dr. John Stauffer—a more than fifty-year run of service by the Stauffers.

A New City Hall

Planning had started for a new city hall as early as 1950. The police and fire departments, along with the water, building and sanitation departments, were housed at 2197 Wilton Drive in a twenty- by sixty-foot office.

In August 1955, the police department was increased to seven employees, and in January 1956, Chief Beaney announced that twenty-four-hour dispatch was available for the water, police and fire departments, with the hiring of P.J. "Tiny" Terrill as night dispatcher. The number to call was Logan 4-1000.[39]

Planning for and achieving a new municipal building was not easy in the 1950s. Location was open to question, and funding was an issue. It was an adventure. There are remarkable parallels with the 2009 construction of a replacement building on Wilton Drive.

Proposed locations included a site on Northeast Twenty-sixth Street at Thirteenth Avenue, on land donated by James Dean and Dave Turner, land that was in proximity to James Dean's proposed Manor Gate shopping center. This had been a main reason for the disagreement with the city council in November 1953.

At the February 1, 1955 council meeting, an offer for land at 543 Northeast Twenty-sixth Street, across the street from the village hall (now the site of the library) was rejected. The council did accept the offer from Dean and Turner on Northeast Twenty-sixth Street, but Dean and Turner wanted construction to start by April 1. A newspaper article shortly after the February 1 vote showed a drawing of a two-story building, designed by Charles McKirahan, at the Dean/Turner site. Construction was supposed to start within two weeks.

The strong opposition to this site by the Wilton Manors Business and Professional Association continued. The association did not want to move the center of town from Wilton Drive.

April 1, 1955, came and went without any construction on the land that Dean and Turner had donated. By September 22, the city had negotiated with J.N. McJunkin for two lots on Northeast Twenty-first Court, on the north side. The purchase price of the two lots, 125 feet long and 95 feet wide, with adjacent parking, was $2,500. The lots had been appraised at $8,000 to $9,000. This deal did not go through.

Negotiations over a site dragged on for months. In July 1956, Food Fair Stores donated a 150- by 250-foot site on the south side of Northeast Twenty-first Court, behind the Atlantic gas station and northwest of the Hagen Park tennis courts, after much cajoling by Al Hagen and other city fathers. The city had recently purchased a 100-square-foot parcel across the street from McJunkin for $3,500 for parking. The city council immediately started planning the building.

The building at the Dean location was designed by Charles McKirahan and was two stories, with a large auditorium upstairs. The Northeast Twenty-first Court building, designed by William F. Bigoney Jr., was also to be two stories, with a two-hundred-seat council chamber, municipal court and community auditorium on the second floor. This plan was rejected as too expensive. On November 28, 1956, the council unofficially decided on a stripped-down version to fit the now $100,000 budget.[40]

Funding was the problem. In December 1953, the city council voted to transfer $10,000 to the new building fund.[41] There were several thousand more dollars in the fund from various sources and promises from several contractors to donate time, labor and materials.

Still, funds were woefully inadequate. Debate started. Should the city tax utilities? Was there sufficient water revenue to back a bond? In February

City hall on Northeast Twenty-first Court, 1959. *WMHS, Stafford.*

1955, the city council voted to authorize an additional $190,000 of water revenue bonds. About 95 percent of this money would go to reimburse developers for installing water distribution pipes. To collect their money, the developers agreed to settle their claims for fifty cents on the dollar. An ad valorem tax referendum had been defeated in September 1954. The projected cost was now $86,000. The tax referendum was approved in 1956.

Finally, in July 1957, the city took possession of the "imposing municipal center."[42] City administrative offices were in the center of the one-story building, flanked by a two-bay fire station at the east end and the police department at the west end. The commission chambers seated about sixty, with standing room. The final cost had crept up to $131,000. There was not enough money left in the budget for furniture. Interior painting, rubber tile flooring, a fire tower, an intercom and numerous other items were not funded. The happiest people when the building opened were the city clerk and the city accountant, both of whom had been working from offices in their homes.

The convoluted back and forth on what was going to be built where and when is further confused by the final address of the new building. The final building was approved to be on Northeast Sixth Avenue and was built there. Except, the newspaper article announcing the "grand opening" had it at 524 Northeast Twenty-first Court. Willingham named the street Choctaw Avenue, and Willingham Jr. changed it to Northeast Twenty-first Court. In 1954, it became Northeast Sixth Avenue, but just before the new city hall opened, the name was changed back to Northeast Twenty-first Court.

STREET NAMES

Street names were specified in the individual development plats, prepared by the various developers.

In the summer of 1954, the city council redesignated a number of streets. Most of those with names were numbered. The notable exceptions were Almar Drive, Coral Gardens Drive and all of Townhouse Isle.

In some cases, the numbered streets or avenues in one subdivision did not line up with the numbers in the adjacent subdivision and were changed. Northeast Twenty-first Court was inexplicably renamed Northeast Sixth Avenue. The folly of this is clear when looking at a map. It was changed back in 1957.

The genius of Willingham's original layout of Wilton Manors is the curve in Wilton Drive. It creates a graceful sweep of an important north-south thoroughfare, which Willingham planned to be residential. Today, it is a reason to pause and pay attention when driving through downtown Wilton Manors. It also makes the street layouts between the drive and Dixie Highway very confusing to residents and visitors to this day.

AD VALOREM TAX

"There wasn't much outcry when taxes had to be levied," Marcia Stafford said. "People knew it was for water and sewers. Besides, it was a small town. Everybody knew everybody and they trusted Dave Turner, Jim Dean, Perry Mickel. And they trusted me, too." The city's first ad valorem property tax—seven mills—took effect on January 1, 1957, having been

Councilman Earle Middleton, former councilman Vernon Burnell, Pat Myers, Kay Noonan, Virginia Van Winkle, Marge Walker, Marie Karsten, Felix Miller, Wally Wakeley, Frank Wolfe and Marcia Stafford (seated), 1958. *WMHS, Stafford.*

approved by the residents the previous November. The total estimated revenue for the city in the fiscal year 1958–59 was $363,000, plus the $66,000 anticipated from the ad valorem tax. Water and sanitation generated $179,000, and the state cigarette tax, another $85,000.

There were some who thought that Wilton Manors should have its own library. In 1957, the Jaycee-ettes, who were backing the movement, were told by the Florida State Library Board chairman that they would need at least $25,000 to start. Enthusiasm trumped capital, and the Jaycee-ettes pressured the other city service clubs to pressure the city council.

Many residents donated books, and Mayor J. Frank Starling donated a tiny key shop in his Manor Market complex in June 1957. On June 14, 1957, the tiny library opened. Kathleen Klein volunteered her services as the first librarian.

UNPLEASANT BUSINESS AND A RECALL ELECTION

In the midst of the completion of the new city hall complex, a crisis erupted involving chief of police Richard Beaney. Marital discord between Beaney and his wife, a school patrol officer, erupted into the public domain and was aired in council chambers and in the pages of the *Fort Lauderdale Daily News*. Rumors circulated, and accusations began.

An "explosive session" of the city council on May 21, 1957, produced two petitions requesting his dismissal. Mayor Starling declared the first to be an "ultimatum": if Beaney were not dismissed, nearly the entire city staff would resign.

Ed Magill, of the *Fort Lauderdale Daily News*, reported boos, catcalls, derisive remarks and arguments that nearly ended in fistfights. Council president Vern Burnell and councilmen Hal Price and Fred Stevens stood their ground and cast the votes to fire Beaney.[43]

Four days later, city clerk Marcia Stafford received an affidavit with the required twenty-five signatures to file a petition for a recall election of the three council members. According to the affidavit, their actions "strike at the very foundations of the democratic form of government," and "this could lead to a totalitarian form of government." These were very strong words during the Cold War.

By June 21, there were enough signatures on the petition to schedule a recall election. The city charter provided for a vote "for" or "against" and a choice of replacement. Mayor Starling left town and went to North Carolina for a vacation.

On June 24, circuit judge Lamar Warren ordered the Wilton Manors City Council to reinstate Beaney. Beaney had argued that his dismissal had not followed either city council or city charter procedures. He also pointed out that he had reported for work on June 12, after a three-week vacation.

By June 28, Marcia Stafford had been named in a lawsuit aimed at shutting down the process of getting the signatures on the petition.

The recall election was held in the middle of August, and Stevens, Price and Burnell won a resounding vote of confidence. Burnell, in his October 1975 oral history recorded for the historical society, was quite emotional about this and felt that the vote of confidence had vindicated him.

Joseph Varon, the city's defense attorney, prevailed by pulling a rabbit out of the legal hat. The 1953 city charter establishing the city of Wilton Manors stated that all appointed and elected officials had to be reappointed. Apparently, Beaney had not been reappointed. He was, therefore, legally terminated when Sergeant Thomas Brace was appointed to the position of chief on June 18, 1957.[44]

Brace had moved to Florida after retiring from the Pennsylvania State Police after twenty-five years. He and his wife, Ethel, had purchased a home on Northeast Twenty-fifth Street, where several other Pennsylvania retirees had bought homes. In March 1956, he had taken the job as a dispatcher for the WMPD. Animal lovers, Brace had a spacious cage for his pet raccoon, and Ethel kept a horse at a ranch on State Road 7 in Lauderhill.

"Tommy" Brace raised the level of professionalism within the police department. He started the police auxiliary, which lasted until 1978, and forged bonds with Oakland Park's police department. Brace was a big supporter of Little League Baseball and a number of other civic activities.

Unfortunately, his tenure was short. He returned from a 1961 trip to the Little League regional championships in Athens, Georgia, with a bad cough. He died later that year.

NEW LIBRARY AND THE BUSIEST YEAR IN HISTORY

That fall, the city took over the library and moved it into the newly vacated town meeting hall. Three years later, the building had doubled in size. By 1960, it contained about ten thousand books and magazines.

In her first column of 1958, Virginia Rogers, who wrote "Wilton Manors Topics" for the *Fort Lauderdale Daily News*, declared 1957

Wilton Manors Library, 1960s. *WMHS.*

A parking problem, 1959. *WMHS.*

one of the busiest, most productive years in Wilton Manors history...1957 saw a continuation of the building boom here. Important commercial additions include three shopping centers...five restaurants, a bowling arena and more than 400 new homes. On January 1, 1957, there were 1,963 water meters here. Today there are 2,358, including at least 1,500 new residents and a total population in excess of 10,000.

The City of Wilton Manors

The columnist's optimistic population estimate had residents looking ahead to the next official census in 1960. What would it show about a village that had grown into a city that was rapidly becoming more complicated?

Buster Barton and Ed Miller opened their dry cleaning establishment at Five Points in 1956. In continuous operation for more than fifty years, Barton and Miller Cleaners is now owned and managed by Ed Miller's son Rick and his wife, Sherry.

Manor Lanes Bowling Center, at 1517 Northeast Twenty-sixth Street, which opened in October 1956, continues to be popular, with numerous active bowling leagues. Al Hagen built nine stores on Wilton Drive in 1956. Manor Way Shopping Center on the 2700 block of Andrews Avenue contained ten stores, and Stevens Market at 2270 Wilton Drive opened in 1957.

On January 14, 1958, a bond issue for $225,000 was approved by the voters for street, sidewalk and storm water sewer construction.

In the "not much changes" department, three days before Christmas 1959, a brand-new 1960 Chrysler New Yorker was driven through the plate glass window of the Little German Bakery at 2287 Wilton Drive. There's no word on whether the driver received a ticket for exceeding the two-hour parking limit or whether ringing the little bells hanging in the window was useful in announcing his arrival.

THE CITY SEAL

The official seal of the City of Wilton Manors depicts the towers designed by Francis Abreu. They were used extensively in publicity about Wilton Manors.

The original seal, adopted by the "Big Meeting" in 1947, was simply a circle with "Wilton" at the top, "Manors" at the bottom and "Seal 1947" in the middle.

The city needed the real thing. J. Frank Starling sketched out the seal from the original arches in the early 1950s.

At some point, the seal was reversed. The larger towers should have been on the left. In 1970, when the fire station vacated city hall and the truck bays became the council chambers, a multicolored cardboard version, complete with sparkles, was installed.

In 1984, council president Diane R. Cline launched a private initiative to re-create the seal in Lucite. Former city council president Vern Burnell pointed out that the image was backward.

Cline hired Hollywood resident Louise Mahoney to re-create the seal. City resident Ruth Bartels began fundraising for the new version, and $750 was raised. The new seal, restored to Starling's original and correct design, was placed behind the city council dais in 1984. It is now behind the dais in the new city hall.

BUILDING OUT

The 1960s

In 1963, Gary Patchen, representing Florida, attended the YMCA Youth Governor Conference in Washington, D.C., and met Attorney General Robert Kennedy, Vice President Lyndon Johnson and Arkansas youth governor Bill Clinton and even danced with actress Jane Mansfield, 1963. *WMHS, Patchen.*

City council meeting, 1962: Marcia Stafford, Gerald McCulley, Frank Starling (city administrator), Harold Price (mayor), George Nichols, John Hanrahan and William Smith, 1962. *WMHS.*

SHOOTING FOR TEN THOUSAND

In her newspaper column, Virginia Rogers had predicted a population of 10,000 by 1960. The 1960 census reported 8,257, still a big jump from 883 in 1950.

To manage the growth, the position of city administrator/manager was created in 1960. The job combined the positions of city clerk, treasurer, purchasing agent and elections supervisor and was filled by J. Frank Starling, who had been mayor for five years.

"I really didn't want it," Starling recalled in 1977. "I took it on a temporary basis until they could get someone else."

Starling, who had served two terms on the city council and two more as mayor, held his "temporary" post for twenty-one years, until he retired in 1981.

The reorganization and the appointment of Starling eliminated Marcia Stafford's position as city clerk, a disappointment to her. After eight years in city government, she used her time well, teaching kindergarten, conducting story hours for children at the library and continuing to make friends for the city. She ran for city council, counting on the votes of people she had served as clerk, and won convincingly, becoming the first woman elected to the city council. Stafford took her seat on January 10, 1961, and held the position for fourteen years and ten months, longer than any council member/commissioner before or after. She resigned two years before her term expired so that her son, Tracy, could run for her seat.

96

SPORTS

Jim McGivern was appointed as city athletics director in 1958. He worked hard to improve recreational facilities at Hagen Park, Mickel Field and the elementary school. He was supported with both public and private funds and oversaw the building of tennis courts at Hagen Park. He created the first golf and tennis teams in the city.

On the Fourth of July 1961, Gary Patchen, age fifteen, drove his sleek, black, gravity-powered Soap Box Derby racer, sponsored by Dixie Lumber, to first place before a crowd of more than fifteen thousand at the Las Olas Bridge. Gary, who lived at 2132 Northwest Fifth Avenue, had raced three times in Fort Lauderdale's All-American Soap Box Derby and had finished fourth, third and second.

"I put a lot of work on my car, but you just can't imagine what it feels like to actually win after coming so close," he said.

Winning brought Gary a huge trophy and a trip to the national championships at Derby Downs in Akron, Ohio.

Before more than 100,000 spectators at the national championships, Gary finished second behind Richard Dawson of Wichita, Kansas. Gary, who had been elected class president three times in high school, was elected youth governor of Florida in 1963. This involved a trip to Washington, D.C., where he met Bill Clinton, who had been elected to the same post in Arkansas. Also part of the festivities were Attorney General Robert Kennedy, Vice President Lyndon Johnson and the incomparable Jayne Mansfield, with whom Gary danced. In the sixty-first derby, in 1998, Gary's son Greg drove a sleek, lean-back racer to second place in the master's division. Daughter Becky also became an accomplished derby racer.

Organized baseball began in 1952. By 1961, the Wilton Manors All-Stars had become the District 7 Little League champs.

Charlie Mitzel coached two generations of Little League Baseball players. To honor his service, the baseball diamond at Mickel Field is dedicated to him.

WAS WILTON MANORS FULL?

On March 4, 1962, reporter Ken Strickland wrote in the *Miami Herald*:

Only 15 years after its incorporation, this central Broward city has nearly reached its saturation point...With 90 percent of the land within its limits now developed, there is little room for additional growth...but residents of the self-contained community could not care less. They pay among the lowest taxes in the county yet have full city services.

The story pointed out that from 1957 through 1961, the total value of new construction had decreased each year. Residential building constituted roughly two-thirds of all construction projects in 1961.

"One effect of the diminishing supply of land has been to enhance the value of existing homes," Mayor Price said. "The value of many of the homes, sold originally for about $15,000, had appreciated to the $18,000 to $24,000 range," the mayor said.

"New families are attracted to the City by its desirable location, shopping and recreation facilities, and, of course, low taxes" the article continued. "Price predicted property in the city will continue to rise in value as long as the community retains its present character. And its contented residents aren't likely to let it change."

THE TOWERS GO

In spite of the hype about the towers in 1925 and 1926, it does not appear that they were universally loved. The largest tower stood empty from 1926 through 1945. M.D. Mace bought the block, including the land behind the pair of towers, in 1944. He

Broward County students on a field trip to Wilton Manors' "castles" in 1929. *WMHS, Blosch.*

remodeled it, adding a bedroom for his son and daughter-in-law. This may have been when a large porch was added to the east side. The Maces were followed by H.L. King, of the Electrolux Corp, and his family. Following the Kings, this tower was the first home of the Wilton Manors Baptist Chapel in 1953.

The towers served as a symbol for the city seal.

The big tower was torn down in April 1957 to make way for an A&W Root Beer drive-in, complete with carhops. The year before, it had been home to a variety of birds, among them twelve parakeets and fifteen valuable mynahs, an owl and two dogs, wards of the "Bird Lady"—or as the sign outside the front door said, "Bird Queen"— Shary O'Hara. She lived with them in the tower, after the Baptist Chapel had vacated, rent-free for two months. O'Hara even posted signs proclaiming the great wonders to be seen inside. When she sold a parakeet and cage to Mrs. Robert Ziawinski, she was arrested for doing business without an occupational license. Court-appointed physicians found O'Hara incompetent to stand trial, and she and her birds were evicted from the "castle" by its owners, Mr. and Mrs. Emet Diamond.

Soon, footage of Shary O'Hara appeared on Ralph Renick's 6:00 p.m. newscast on Miami's WTVJ. "Not the Bird Queen moving because the building is being torn down, but rather the building torn down to move Mrs. O'Hara," Renick quipped. Mrs. O'Hara stood her ground for two more days on the Wilton Drive sidewalk.

Some effort was made to maintain the remaining towers. The windows were boarded up, and at least the northwestern pair was painted white in 1955. Some time prior to that, a telephone booth had been installed directly in front of the northwest pair.

An article in the *Miami Herald*, written by Ray Linders and Don Bedwell about 1964, announced that the northwest towers were going to be torn down to make way for a gas station. There seems to have been more concern about "why do we need another gas station?" and the nesting sparrows than about preserving a historic landmark.

"It's wicked to take it down with all those birds in it," a resident told the *Miami Herald*. "There are hundreds of sparrows in there—it's something of a bird sanctuary."

The tower came down, but the city, home to flocks of parrots since 1952, softened the blow by declaring Wilton Manors a bird sanctuary.

The article makes several mentions that the towers had not been maintained, and they were probably targets for vandalism. In the article, Frank Starling, the city administrator, said that there were no plans to tear down the final tower next to the A&W Root Beer stand, but the article ends on a pessimistic note.

The last tower was, in fact, torn down about 1964. Wilton Drive was widened to make a right-turn lane south onto Dixie Highway at Five Points.

MORE PROGRESS

By 1965, Mayor Price reported that city household and voter registration statistics indicated the population had reached 10,000. There were 4,867 registered voters.

Three main arteries serving Wilton Manors were being widened and improved, the mayor reported. Oakland Park Boulevard and Andrews Avenue were being expanded to four lanes, and sidewalks were being completed. Old Dixie Highway was being widened.

Saint Nicholas Orthodox Church on Andrews Avenue was founded in the early 1960s, and Hurricane Cleo hit in 1964.

The Robinson Beauty School was built in 1965 on Northeast Twenty-sixth Street by the world-renowned architect Dan Duckham. The building was later the headquarters of the Boys and Girls Club of Broward County. In 2006, it was purchased by Louis Shuster (who had coveted it for years) and was completely

Harold Price, circa 1965. *WMHS.*

Building Out

Advertisement for Robinson Beauty School, 1966. *WMHS, Ulm.*

renovated to become his design studio. The historical society recognized Mr. Shuster and the importance of his restoration of the building with an award.

Manor Pines, a skilled nursing and rehabilitation center on Northeast Twenty-sixth Street, was opened in 1966 by Ralph Marrison.

Kathleen Klein, Wilton Manors' librarian since the library's start in 1957, retired in 1966. Mary Jane Schmidt was named library director, a position she held for eighteen years.

That summer, Grace and Robert Newton opened their pink, seven-bedroom home to four children with developmental disabilities. They were aided in their work by the Broward County Association for Retarded Children and the Wilton Manors Baptist Church.

"We've never had any children of our own," Grace Newton said. "When we decided to open our home to the mentally retarded, we had no training in the field. But it's been the turning point in our lives."

The Newtons named their home the Turning Point, the Newton Home for Special Children.

"When we built here in 1947, Wilton Manors was still pioneer country," Grace Newton said.

There were just a few gravel roads, a lot of rattlesnakes and about fifty people in the whole area. We helped organize a civic association and two churches. I became a charter member of the Wilton Manors Woman's Club and worked with the Girl Scouts. I watched Wilton Manors change from a village to a city. Two years ago, we felt that our work in the community was finished...then a neighbor spoke to us about taking in mentally retarded children. We accepted the challenge.

In the spring of 1966, Harold Gair, Wilton Manors' third police chief, resigned for health reasons, and Captain Felix Miller was appointed to serve as acting chief while the city looked for a candidate to fill a job that was becoming more demanding as the population of the city and the surrounding area swelled. Mayor Price and the city council promoted from within, picking Bernard Scott, the candidate who had scored highest in a competitive examination.

Scott was hired as a patrol officer in 1958, promoted to sergeant in 1963 and then became captain. When he assumed the position of chief in 1966, he was, at thirty, the youngest police chief in Florida. He served with distinction for twenty-three years, until 1989.

Also in January, Mayor Price died after a short illness. He was fifty-nine. A native of Pennsylvania, Price had come to the city with his family to operate a gas station on Wilton Drive and became active in politics and community service. At the time of his death, Price was a jail steward at the Broward County Sheriff's Office. He served on the city council from 1956 to 1960 and as mayor from 1960 until his death. He was also president of the Broward County League of Municipalities, a member of the Wilton Manors Kiwanis Club, a volunteer fireman and former president of the Wilton Manors Chamber of Commerce.

Elected to succeed Price was Gerald Thompson, who went on to play a major role in Wilton Manors and Broward County. A former bartender and swimming pool contractor, Thompson had been elected to the city council in 1964. He served as mayor until 1974.

In 1960, John Miller, owner of a radio-TV repair shop on Northeast Sixth Avenue, became the city's sixth volunteer fire chief. Father of five and known to most as "Coach," he served as chief for twenty years, turning the reins over to Richard Rothe in 1980. In 1972, he closed his repair shop for good and became the city's first paid fire marshal in addition to his volunteer role as fire chief.[45]

A new fire station was built on Northeast Twenty-second Street in 1969, freeing space at city hall for a larger commission chambers.

In March 1968, the new faces on the city council were Eugene Metzger and James Maurer. Each would become mayor in the 1970s.

In 1968, the city council authorized the city's first sewer revenue bond issue in the amount of $1.5 million. This was a milestone in converting the city's septic tank system to a modern sewer system to accommodate the city's residential and commercial growth.

A QUIET TIME

The 1970s

City council, 1970: William Smith (council), William Miller (city attorney), Frank Starling (city administrator), James Maurer (council), Marcia Stafford (council), Gerald Thompson (mayor), Eugene Metzger (council) and Marvin Meecham (council). *WMHS.*

Vol. 7, No. 3   1550 N.E. 26th STREET, FT. LAUDERDALE, FLA. 33305   March, 1973

AT LAST! LUNDE TOWERS IS UNDER CONSTRUCTION

Artist's rendering of Lunde Towers, to be located in Wilton Manors on South Fork of Middle River.

GROUND BREAKING

The official "Ground Breaking" for Lunde Towers was held on Sunday, February 18, 1973. The site is one of the most attractive in Broward County, covered with magnificent cypress trees, wild orchids and beautiful birds. Located at the entrance to Town House Isle sequestered off from Wilton Drive, the arbor of trees guard the entry to this lovely spot.

Officiating at the "Ground Breaking" ceremony were Mr. William Passalaqua, Al Hagen, Worthy Seese, Dr. Lunde, Mayor Gerald Thompson and city council members Arthur Welling and Marsha Stafford. The apartment

Continued on Page 2

A scene at the "Ground Breaking" — church members and city dignitaries join for the exciting event.

Church of Religious Science newsletter, 1973. *WMHS.*

BREAKING TEN THOUSAND AND REBUFFING A SUITOR

A population of 10,000 had been predicted since 1960, but the 1970 census finally confirmed 10,948.

As Wilton Manors grew, so did Fort Lauderdale and Oakland Park. We were turning into a "greater metropolitan area," with more traffic and more crime.

By the early 1970s, Fort Lauderdale was again casting covetous eyes at Wilton Manors. In the *Town Crier* newsletter, Mayor Thompson sent out an appeal to "save our city." To persuade residents to oppose a takeover by Fort Lauderdale, he called for them to support Wilton Manors in a straw vote in the March 19, 1971 elections. The mayor wrote:

A Quiet Time

Perhaps the 11ᵗʰ Commandment should be—"Thou shalt not covet thy neighbor's municipal treasury." The power structure of our southern neighbor [Fort Lauderdale] *is again requesting the Legislature to abolish Wilton Manors. We would then share in the cost of Fort Lauderdale's past and future inefficiency, with a minority voice in decisions.*

The voters said decisively that they preferred to remain independent—a town of their own. In addition, from a field of eleven candidates, they reelected Marcia Stafford, with 1,509 votes, and elected Arthur Welling, with 656 votes, for his first term on the council. In 1976, Welling, a Realtor, was elected mayor, a position he held for four years.

In 1971, George Richardson Jr. sold much of his father's old golf course bordering Andrews Avenue. The Manor Grove condominiums were built there between 1971 and 1973. With about six hundred residences, built in four phases, it remains Wilton Manors' largest residential complex.

The Church of Religious Science was established on Northeast Twenty-sixth Street and Northeast Fifteenth Avenue in 1972. Lunde Towers, now Wilton Towers, Wilton Manors' tallest building at eleven stories, was built by the church as a luxury retirement rental residence for members of the church at the south end of Wilton Drive. One- and two-bedroom apartments ranged from 679 to 1,040 square feet, with rents between $215 and $330 a month. It was subsequently turned into rental apartments available to all.

CRIME IN THE ISLAND CITY

In December 1971, Gerard John Schaefer Jr. was hired by the Wilton Manors Police Department. Schaefer had graduated from Florida Atlantic University and from the Broward County Police Academy at Broward Community College. The soft-spoken, baby-faced Schaefer was fired six months later for hanging a drunken man upside down beneath a bridge. Chief Scott noted that the young officer had "some very strange ideas about law enforcement."

Schaefer was hired by the Martin County Sheriff's Department in June 1972. In July, he was fired for having gagged and handcuffed a pair of female hitchhikers to trees on Hutchinson Island. One of the women freed herself and ran for help, forcing Schaefer to confess to Martin County sheriff Robert Crowder that he had done something "very foolish." Schaefer was fired, arrested and charged with aggravated assault.

The next year, he was convicted for the mutilation murders of Susan Place and Georgia Jessup, both of Oakland Park, on Hutchinson Island.

Schaefer ultimately was suspected of as many as twenty-eight murders. He was stabbed to death in a fight on December 3, 1995, over a cup of hot water.

Chief Scott subsequently pushed successfully for psychological testing for all WMPD job applicants.

In any community, murder is tragedy. Fourteen-year-old William Smith returned to his home in June 1973 to find his mother and siblings shot and stabbed to death. In 1978, Joyce "Cookie" Summerhill was raped and murdered while walking south on Andrews Avenue to Big Daddy's Lounge, just over the river in Fort Lauderdale. Her partially decomposed body was found a week later.

One of the strangest offenders in Wilton Manors was a 1972 Chevrolet Impala.

Joe Velasco was using his blue-and-white Chevy to jump-start a neighbor's car. When the car finally started, the neighbor climbed out, and Velasco attempted to disconnect the cables. The car popped into gear and began driving in circles on the 2700 block of Northeast First Way.

Ana Maria Fenimore, staff writer for the *Fort Lauderdale News*, went into overdrive on her Smith Corona, putting the "pedal to the metal" with her coverage of the incident.

Headlines read "Re-inCARnation in Wilton Manors" and "Joe's Chevy Survives Shootout." Fenimore's report read:

> ...in a scene reminiscent of the movie "Bonnie and Clyde."
> When the Abbott and Costello-style foot race failed, a fire truck was called in hopes of drowning the runaway into submission.
> Police Lt. Perry Hempstead...gave the fateful order to fire when it became obvious the car's career would end—violently—in someone's carport...
> Four shotgun blasts into the gaping hood ended the affair.
> "And now everybody asks us all the time if we shoot Fords," Hempstead said. "I think I'm ready to move into the office for a while." The Chevy, after $400 worth of repairs, recovered.

Crime in a small community is personal. Wilton Manors has been the victim of "spill over" from Fort Lauderdale and Oakland Park. Back in 1950, when Floyd Miller was given his police car and a radio, residents were proud of their police force. Today's police department has modern technology and practices. With its new headquarters, it is fully accredited, employs state-of-the-art equipment and business practices and enjoys the continued support of residents.

CITY COMMISSION AS A STEPPINGSTONE

The Wilton Manors City Council has been a steppingstone to important positions with Broward County, the Florida House and even mayor of Fort Lauderdale.

Gerald Thompson was a city commissioner from 1964 to 1968 and then mayor from 1968 to 1974. In 1974, he was elected to the Broward County Commission, a post he held for twenty-two years—a county record. He was chairman of the commission on four occasions—also a record. He was also chairman of the Broward County Expressway Authority, creator of the Sawgrass Expressway.

James E. Maurer succeeded Thompson as mayor. A physical education teacher at Fort Lauderdale High School, he served three terms as mayor before resigning when he was appointed superintendent of Broward County's schools on August 23, 1975. He remained in that position until June 30, 1979.

Colohatchee Park Boardwalk, 2009. *WMHS, Little.*

Named to succeed Maurer on Wilton Manors' council was Eugene Metzger, who, with his brother Philip, developed Deer Creek in Deerfield Beach. Metzger, a native of Columbus, Ohio, had attended graduate school at the University of Miami. He served six terms on the Wilton Manors City Council, but although his tenure as mayor was less than a year, it left him with fond memories.

"There were very few problems in those days," said Metzger, a Jenada Isle resident. "The city was not burdened with indebtedness, the town had a strong tax base and we had no appreciable crime or density problems. People genuinely liked the town. It was a great time and a great community to raise a family."

Metzger held office at the midpoint of the decade, and it turned out to be a high point. For the city, 1974 was a very good year. Some four hundred businesses were operating, and the city was home to six churches, two grammar schools, service clubs and Boy Scout and Girl Scout troops. Of the city's 5,916 residences, 2,740 were single-family homes, 540 duplexes, 2,467 condominiums and 169 mobile homes. The estimated population of the city was fifteen thousand, but the next two official censuses had it much lower.

In 1975, Colohatchee Natural Park opened on the South Fork of Middle River at Northeast Fifteenth Avenue. The park offered visitors a journey into six and a half acres of unspoiled mangrove swamp harking back to the days before Willingham. Land for the park had been purchased in 1972 with an $85,000 grant from the federal government's Open Space Land Program and a $10,000 grant from the Florida Department of Natural Resources.

Elevated boardwalks led through the red and black mangroves into a world of birds, raccoons, crabs and butterflies, even an occasional alligator. Supplementing the natural amenities were picnic tables, play areas and a boat ramp at Northeast Fifteenth Avenue.

CITY PARKS

Population growth, good sense and legal requirements for open space have all driven the development of city parks. Funding has come from gifts, city monies, bond issues and grants from the federal, state and county governments. The voter-approved $3 million bond issue of November 1998 was a significant factor in making the newer parks possible.

A Quiet Time

Willingham promised five beautiful parks. To date, the City of Wilton Manors has delivered eleven beautiful parks, plus a large number of little respites where butterflies and birds enjoy native plants, provided by city and volunteer labor.

The adventurous may rent a kayak and stop at Richardson, Colohatchee, ICPP, Eisele and Snook Creek Parks on a morning or afternoon circumnavigation of Wilton Manors.

The WILTON MANORS ELEMENTARY SCHOOL BALL FIELD is officially a Wilton Manors park. Opened in 1952, it was upgraded with the 1998 parks bond monies. At 2401 Northeast Third Avenue, it is the site of a number of annual events and hosts many league events. It is leased from the county.

HAGEN PARK, the site of Alvar Hagen's golf driving range at 2020 Wilton Drive, is a 5.2-acre complex with tennis and basketball courts and a large community center. The park opened in 1955, on land donated to the city by Hagen. It has undergone several renovations since. It is the headquarters for the city's Leisure Services Department and the prime location for city-sponsored indoor and outdoor events. It is also the venue for city commission meetings too large to fit in the chambers at city hall—a tribute to Al Hagen's civic foresight.

MICKEL FIELD is at the western end of the city at 2675 Northwest Seventh Avenue. It is a 4.9-acre athletic complex, including lighted baseball fields and a multipurpose building with a concession stand. The land belonged to Perry Mickel, who, in 1955, leased it to Wilton Manors Sports, Inc., for $1 a year. The city purchased the land for $21,000 in 1960.

JAYCEE PARK occupies the funny little triangle forced by Wilton Drive, Northeast Fifth Avenue and Northeast Twenty-third Street. It is a nice spot to sit and relax when "walking the drive." Dating from the 1960s, it has recently undergone a major renovation.

CORAL GARDENS PARK, on Coral Gardens Drive, is a "pocket park," a good spot to stop during an evening walk and chat with neighbors, also on their evening walks. Formally named in the 1970s, it is a small triangle formed by Coral Gardens Drive and Northeast Twenty-seventh Street.

RACHEL RICHARDSON PARK is a quiet corner on the busy Andrews Avenue and Northeast Twenty-first Court. It was a gift to the city from Judge George Richardson Jr. in honor of his mother in 1968.

COLOHATCHEE PARK, at 1975 Northeast Fifteenth Avenue, is the largest park in Wilton Manors, at 8.5 acres. It was purchased in 1972 and opened in 1975. It is accessed over a boardwalk through mangroves on the South Fork of the Middle River. It was upgraded in 1998 and again in 2001 and 2005. The park straddles Northeast Fifteenth Avenue. On the east side of the avenue is a boat ramp to the South Fork of the Middle River with additional guest facilities.

ISLAND CITY PARK PRESERVE, at 823 Northeast Twenty-eighth Street, was an addition to Kiwanis Park, developed in the mid-1990s, and is located on a private part of the North Fork of the Middle River in Highland Estates. It was dedicated in September 2003. When sitting on the boardwalk, overlooking the North Fork of the Middle River, one can imagine what Colohatchee might have been like in Collier's time. It is about three acres. During Prohibition, moonshiners set up camp near here on two uninhabited islands, where they operated illegal whiskey stills.

DONN EISELE PARK, at 701 Northwest Twenty-ninth Street, is a one-acre jewel on the site of the old Jenada Swimming Pool. There is boat access to the North Fork of the Middle River. It was opened in 2001. An entrance to the Jenada Villas subdivision was uncovered here and has been restored by the Westside Association of Wilton Manors.

RICHARDSON HISTORIC PARK AND NATURE PRESERVE, 5.4 acres at 1937 Wilton Drive, is the former home of Judge George Richardson Jr., the site of part of his father's golf course and the Willingham's house before that. It was purchased in 2002 with county and state grants and money from the 1998 parks bond. The Manor House is available for rentals. There is a large outdoor pavilion, a nature walk and a boat dock on the South Fork of the Middle River.

SNOOK CREEK PARK is a half-acre boat launch at 2351 Powerline Road and the South Fork of the Middle River. It opened in 2009. It reminds people entering and leaving Wilton Manors on Powerline Road that this is the "Island City."

M.E. DEPALMA PARK, at the corner of Northeast Seventh Avenue and Northeast Twentieth Drive is the newest "pocket park." It honors the work of Ms. M.E. DePalma in getting Wilton Manors designated as a Community Wildlife Habitat by the National Wildlife Federation, the seventeenth city in the nation to be so honored.

A Quiet Time

In 1975, the Wilton Manors Historical Society held its first membership meeting at city hall on September 15. President Dianne Thompson, wife of Gerald Thompson, presented honorary lifetime memberships to Merle Slagle, Grace Newton, Alvar Hagen and city attorney William Miller for his work in drafting and obtaining the city's charter. The historical society taped interviews with a number of pioneers.

Marcia Stafford, one of the city's most long-serving political leaders, stepped down. Elected to the seat she vacated was her son, Tracy.

Tracy Stafford, circa 1988. *WMHS.*

In 1976, Arthur Welling, who had served on the city council since March 1971, succeeded Gene Metzger as mayor. Joining him on the council were Jack Zeman and Sandra Jedlicka, administrative assistant to Broward County property appraiser William Markham. Jedlicka had come to Florida in 1957. In 1978, she married Robert Steen.

In May 1975, city council president Sam Stevens reported that the 22,256-square-foot Food Fair supermarket at 2020 Wilton Drive was going out of business. The building and its adjacent 4.5 acres were for sale for $550,000. Stevens urged his nervous colleagues to take steps to purchase the property.

At the time, the prescient Stevens said: "Twenty years from now this is going to seem like a good deal we missed, if we miss it now." The purchase was consummated the following year. For $429,426, it included four and a half acres of land and the building at 2020 Wilton Drive, containing 22,256 square feet of floor area. The property's appraised value was $540,000.

"Your City Council feels that the acquisition of this property is essential in order to provide for the needs of the City now and in the future," wrote council president Fred B. Fetzer in the *Town Crier.* Possible future uses included a new, expanded public library, municipal parking, city office space and expanded recreation and park facilities.

REVOLUTION

The 1980s

Wednesday, March 3, 1982

Page 4

The TRIBUNE

Opin

Manors meeting

...or Editor:

...ed in W   By Ellen Stein

Drive to weaken mayor's powers starts in Manors

Manors feud escalates as

₁f system
oo much

Opposing groups do about-faces

Thursday, September 20, 1984 / The Miami Herald   9BR

force opposing ballot ques...

...would
to settle

— Jane Carroll,
elections
supervisor

Battle lines drawn and redrawn. *WMHS, Little.*

QUIET START TO A THREE-RING CIRCUS

The 1980 census was a disappointment. It reported a population of 12,718, well below the anticipated 15,000 in 1975. With Jim Maurer regaining his seat as mayor in 1980, the city was approaching "build out."

Even though development was beginning to cool off, the 1980s were to be very exciting politically, with warring civic groups, questionable hiring of full-time staff and significant changes to the form of government.

Festering since 1978 was the appointment of a Charter Review Board to review the city charter, first adopted in 1953. The council agreed to appoint one in September 1978 but did not do so until January 1982.

Tensions began building in January 1979, when the council hired Sam Stevens to be the city's chief building inspector, effective the following summer. Stevens was a sitting member of the council. Mayor Arthur Welling, who had been openly feuding with Stevens for several months, claimed that this violated the city's civil service regulations and that the city council had acted illegally.

As reported by the *Fort Lauderdale News* on January 10, 1979, city attorney William G. Miller said that he would require at least two weeks to research the law. "The debate also was spiced by an exchange of acid comments and ridiculing statements."[46] Residents in attendance at the council meeting were disturbed. Former council member Vernon Burnell observed, "This doesn't seem to be the same city as when I sat on the council." Another resident observed that recent council meetings had come to resemble a "three-ring circus."

Two weeks later, city officials and lawyers still had not been able to determine what the civil service regulations stated. The regulations that were approved by council resolution on November 13, 1973, could not be found. There were no minutes of the Civil Service Board to be found in the city records.

In February, the state attorney general ruled that the appointment of Stevens as a full-time, paid city employee was contrary to public policy, against good conscience and public morals and should be held void. In March, the city attorney ruled that the attorney general's ruling was invalid. The council then elected Stevens as president of the city council.

Stevens is an ambiguous character, much loved by several longtime city employees who worked with him and an easy object of ridicule based on published reports of the activities of the time.

In 1981, Frank Starling retired after twenty-one years as city administrator. The second move from the dais to a full-time city job was in September. Tracy Stafford, who had resigned his seat on the council, was hired as city administrator over some sixty other candidates and loud objections from a packed council chamber.

To fill Stafford's seat, the council picked a newcomer to town: Donn Eisele. The command module pilot for *Apollo 7*, Eisele had moved to Jenada Isle earlier in the year. He had served as a director of the Peace Corps in Thailand and was a stockbroker for Oppenheimer & Co. As a resident of the western part of the city, the council looked to him to fill a void in representation.

Said Eisele of his job on the Wilton Manors City Council: "I don't know what's on the horizon."

More questions arose about the qualifications of full-time city employees. In June 1980, John Ciullo was appointed acting finance director when Steve Wood resigned. In October 1981, the Civil Service Board discovered that Wood did not have the educational credentials required. This became a hot topic in the newspapers.

A letter to the editor of the *Tribune* on November 18, 1981, was headlined, "Wilton Manors Stirring." It was.

THE BATTLE LINES ARE DRAWN

October 1981 saw Bob DuBree and his wife, Barbara, organizing "concerned" citizens under the reconstituted banner of the Wilton Manors Civic Association. DuBree and his wife opted not to seek officers' posts in the new organization because they had become "too controversial."[47]

Cline and Turner campaign material, 1982. *WMHS.*

By the beginning of 1982, the lines had been drawn between the "Old Guard" and the "New Guard." There was a demand to end cronyism. The city budget had been increased substantially in October 1981, arousing protests of higher property taxes.

There were seven candidates for the two city council positions in the March 9 election. Incumbents Donn Eisele and Sandy Jedlicka faced off against Bill Turner, acting president of the Civic Association, and Diane R. Cline, vice-president of the Civic Association, as well as three others. Turner was the general manager of Taylor and Turner Pest Control, the grandson of Dave Turner, Wilton Manors' first mayor. Cline had moved to Wilton Manors with her husband and five children from Ohio in 1977.

Turner and Cline ran as a ticket, sharing both expenses and the message of change. Much to the surprise of many residents, they won. A city charter amendment was also approved, calling for the annual election of a council president instead of one every other year after the general election.

POWER SHIFTS

At their first council meeting, Turner and Cline were joined by Jack Zeman, first elected in 1976, in voting to terminate William G. Miller, who had been city attorney for thirty years. Morris C. Tucker was appointed to replace him.

They voted to not reappoint city manager Tracy Stafford, treasurer John Cuillo and city clerk Debbie Basone, placing them on probation for sixty days so that the new council could take more time to evaluate their performance.

The tone set in the campaign was now set in cement. There were six votes that night where the vote was three to two. Zeman said of Cline and Turner, "I think they have ideas that should be listened to" and pointed out that they had campaigned door-to-door and spoken to many people who agreed with their positions.[48]

During the campaign, one of the big issues was whether or not the city needed its own building department. Sam Stevens, the former council member and president of the council and now building director, tried to push the issue on whether or not he was going to be fired.

Expecting that the council was going to fire them, Stafford and Stevens resigned. Both Cuillo and Basone were rehired by unanimous vote. Cuillo's title was changed to comptroller, to account for his experience making up for his academic credentials. Basone resigned on July 20, amid allegations of having abused telephone privileges, to pursue a career as an opera and gospel singer and because of "political pressures."[49]

Revolution

In the summer of 1982, Michael Curran resigned from the council to run for the state legislature. In a move that smacked of the same cronyism they had campaigned against, the Turner, Cline and Zeman faction voted to appoint Loren "Duke" Maltby to complete Curran's term. Mayor Maurer vetoed the decision in favor of holding an election. The council was unable to override the veto. The city attorney said the veto was legal. Then he said it was not. The state attorney general agreed that the veto was not legal; this time, the city attorney respected the ruling. The council again voted to appoint Maltby and succeeded.

Meanwhile, the city had no administrator. With the loss of key personnel, no administrator and no consensus on what the role of administrator should be, newspapers were suggesting that Wilton Manors was completely out of control. All the factions insisted that this was untrue.

The mayor proposed a candidate for administrator. The council wanted to interview all the finalists. J. Scott Miller, city manager of East Detroit, Michigan—and not the mayor's choice—was selected as the first city manager with professional credentials. He would serve in this capacity for three years. His appointment by the new city council not only helped precipitate the city charter change in 1984, but it also brought a new professionalism to the city staff and its procedures.

The years 1982 and 1983 were rocky, with letters to the editor complaining about rudeness at public meetings. There were frequent newspaper articles about the unrest. The "Old Guard" formed the Concerned Citizens of Wilton Manors to counter the influence of the Civic Association. The Concerned Citizens showed up one night at a meeting of the Civic Association in an attempted coup. On a positive side, plans were made to double the size of the police department headquarters at the west end of city hall.

Cline was elected council president in August 1982 and, to her surprise, was reelected to the position in March 1984. The new city charter abolished the position in November 1984. At that time, she became the city's first vice-mayor.

Diane R. Cline, circa 1982. *WMHS, Cline.*

In a bizarre turn, Cline was briefly acting mayor. In late June 1983, Mayor Maurer failed to attend a scheduled council meeting. He had not been seen at city hall for a week and, according to press accounts, had not left word that he would be away. The *Miami Herald* reported that his home had been for sale for weeks and that his phone had been disconnected.[50] (The *Miami Herald* story was the four-column lead on the "regional" section. Directly below the story was a four-column photo of two gorillas looking puzzled and scratching their heads. A comment on Wilton Manors politics? Below the fold, the caption made clear that human officials at the Miami Metrozoo did not understand the love life of gorillas. The juxtaposition must have been coincidental.) Officials were concerned enough to seek a legal opinion on when the office would be declared vacant.

As council president, Cline became acting mayor and thus was not able to vote on the council, significantly shifting an uneasy balance of power on the council. Cline signed the authorizations to keep the government machinery running. After two weeks, Maurer telephoned city administrator Scott Miller to tell him he had been taking a vacation.

"A guy can't even take a vacation without somebody looking for him," Maurer complained. A July 11, 1983 editorial in the *Fort Lauderdale News* chastised him for his unannounced two-week absence. The city council was embroiled in a messy and expensive fight over city employee pensions, and a key vote to settle the issue failed because Cline could not vote.

A June 1983 editorial in the *Miami Herald*, headlined "Manors Mess Proves Need to Get Serious," opened by saying, "The Wilton Manors pension mess continues to deepen. With each succeeding disclosure, one can only ask, in wonderment, how the city managed to foul up things so badly."[51]

1984: WHO IS ELECTED TO WHAT?

The ballot in March 1984 presented a number of open questions. The November 1984 ballot had the potential to plunge the city into a morass reminiscent of Dickens's *Bleak House*. Straight-faced, 180-degree turns were rampant.

The city charter was finally reviewed, and a vote to change it was scheduled to coincide with the March 1984 council and mayoral election.

The mayor's race came down to Robert DuBree, a primary force in resuscitating the 1946 Civic Association as "the new guard" (who had not run in 1981 because he and his wife had "become too controversial"), versus Sam Stevens, who had earlier resigned as chief building inspector and was now a city building official in Tamarac.

Revolution

Newspaper profiles of candidates at the time listed "age," "education," "experience" and "quotation" along with a picture of the candidates. Occupation was not specified. DuBree was something of a mystery. An article in the *Sun-Sentinel*, in its March 6, 1984 endorsement of candidates, recommended Bob Dubree. He "owns and manages an apartment complex in the city."[52] City fire inspection records indicate that the property at 2209 Northeast Twenty-sixth Street belonged to DuBree and was called Point Rio. It is now the Cabanas Guest House.

On March 6, 1984, the *News and Sun-Sentinel* endorsed DuBree, Ruth Bartels and incumbent James Grady. Bartels was supported by the Civic Association, but the *News and Sun-Sentinel* thought that the Concerned Citizens' support of Grady would bring a much-needed balance. This was the equivalent of endorsing a cobra and a mongoose.

One of the changes to the city charter was significant. To this point, there was a five-member city council, elected to staggered four-year terms every other year. The council elected a president and a vice-president. There was also a mayor who did not have a vote on the council but could veto their decisions. Council members were responsible for various aspects of city management; there were police and road commissioners. In addition, the city administrator was responsible for the daily operation of the city. The ballot question on the charter change would shorten the mayor's term from four years to two, make him a member of the five-member city council and take away his veto.

Because of this ballot question, it was difficult to determine who would win the election. If the question passed, the top two vote-getters for council would win because the candidate who won for mayor would take the third open seat on the council. If the question were defeated, the top three vote-getters would be appointed, and the mayor would continue as a separate entity, with veto power.

The question was defeated. Wayne W. Musgrave Jr., president-elect of the Oakland Park/Wilton Manors Chamber of Commerce, and Marvin Bush, a retired Sears manager and salesman, received the most votes. They had been endorsed by Stevens. James Grady came in third and thus was seated. Bartels came in fourth.

When the votes for mayor were counted, Stevens had 1,606 and DuBree trailed with 1,517. But because Florida was a "resign to run" state, Floyd Rogers, a resident, announced he would take legal action to remove Stevens from the ballot since he was an official of another municipality. By the time a Broward Circuit Court judge disqualified Stevens, it was too late to remove his name from the ballot. As the only candidate who was legally in the race, DuBree became the mayor.

It is hard to imagine a more politically charged alignment of city charter, mayor and council.

The newly elected Musgrave and Bush joined reelected incumbent James Grady, pushing Turner and Cline into the minority.

City attorney Morris C. Tucker, who had replaced William G. Miller (who had been fired at the first council meeting after the 1982 election), suffered the same fate at the first council meeting after the March 1984 election.

Alan Ruf was appointed acting city attorney. Mayor DuBree vetoed the appointment. James A. Cherof of Josias and Goren was hired, again with a three-to-two vote, with Mayor DuBree threatening to veto again. DuBree had supported the charter amendment, which deprived the mayor of veto power, but when he had it, he did not hesitate to use it.

The council held emergency meetings. Broward Circuit Court judges were making rulings and suspending them. Recall campaigns and citizen lawsuits were threatened. Cherof lasted until November, and Tucker was back.

The bad blood between the two factions even spilled over into a battle over who would be granted the beer concession at the city's 1984 Fourth of July celebration: the chamber of commerce or the Jaycees. Happily, a compromise was reached and temperance avoided.

ELECTION "DO-OVER" AND A NEW CHARTER

Everyone was unhappy with the March results on the charter amendment. Donn Eisele, who had been defeated by Diane Cline and Bill Turner in 1982, wanted to put the question back on the ballot in November. Eisele stated that he was "very concerned about the state of affairs in our government."

Eisele contended, perhaps correctly, that the mayor had too much power. In the past, he said, this arrangement "has always worked because we've had laid-back, easy-going mayors." Not anymore.

Eisele's charter amendment proposal—listed on the ballot as "Charter Amendment"—put the mayor on the council with a vote and no veto. The key was that the mayor and vice-mayor would be elected by the council. If this measure passed, DuBree was out. The five council members would serve staggered four-year terms, slowing radical shifts in direction.

A competing proposal—listed on the ballot as the "People's Proposal"—was essentially the one that had been defeated in March. It called for a mayor elected by the people to a two-year term and the balance of the council to staggered four-year terms. This would allow for quicker changes in direction. As in Eisele's proposal, the mayor did not have a veto.

Revolution

Both proposals invested significant and specific power in the city manager, who would effectively be the chief executive officer.

Impossibly, both proposals appeared on the ballot, not as "either/or" but as "yes /no" on both. County supervisor of elections Jane Carroll had no idea what would happen if both passed.

"A judge would have to settle it…First of all, you're not supposed to put two diametrically opposed proposals on the ballot because you can't have two forms of government," she said in the October 4, 1984 *Fort Lauderdale News*.[53]

The People's Proposal passed 68 percent to 32 percent. The other proposal lost, 45 percent to 55 percent. At least some of the voters must have been confused by the wording.

Wayne Musgrave, who had the fewest votes of the three winners in March, should have relinquished his seat but refused. His lawyer told the council, "We want the record to reflect [Musgrave] isn't leaving any of his council rights."[54] Tracy Stafford had filed a lawsuit to get what turned out to be the winning proposition removed from the ballot. He lost but was appealing. The council certified the results but voted not to send them to the state, as required by Florida law. Mayor DuBree sent them on his own authority anyway.

The balance of power changed again in March 1986. Attorney Tucker was out again, to be temporarily replaced by fifty-year resident George Richardson Jr. Cherof returned, and the city continues to be represented by Cherof's successor firm, Goren, Cherof, Doody and Ezrol, PA.

OTHER EXCITEMENT

Not all of the excitement was political. On a May night in 1980, Wilton Manors police received a report that a high-powered, Excalibur-type boat had docked at a home in the 2400 block of Northeast Eighteenth Avenue, on the South Fork of the Middle River. A large number of people crept from the boat and entered the house. Five police officers, including future police chief Steve Kenneth, surrounded it.

In early afternoon, police and border patrol officers arrested three smugglers and fourteen Colombian immigrants. The Colombians had been smuggled from Bimini for $600 to $800 each.

At 276 pounds, the muscular six-foot-two Mayor Maurer was "overweight." Cecil Nall, director of parks and recreation, came up with a plan—not just for the mayor but for everyone battling a weight problem. In conjunction with the American Heart Association and the Broward County Dietetic Association, he formed the Wilton Manors Lose-a-Ton Club. Nearly three hundred men and women signed up for the program, including Mayor Maurer.

Diets were tailored to each participant, and weekly weigh-ins and seminars were offered to motivate club members to continue sensible eating. Club members received discount cards for health food stores. Health clubs and the recreation department offered special exercise sessions. At the halfway point, the group's total weight loss was just short of five hundred pounds.

The final weigh-in was November 21, 1981, at city hall. About 250 of the original 300 participants showed up. The total number of pounds lost was 2,087, just enough to claim success. Still, the effort wasn't over. Other members came in within a few days to weigh in, and the total weight lost rose to 2,340, an average of 8 pounds per participant. The person who trimmed off the most weight was the mayor, who lost 38 pounds. In the wake of the program's success, people began wearing T-shirts emblazoned with "Wilton Manors—The Town That Lost a Ton" all over town.

Nall launched the program to "get the town healthy" because he had been diagnosed with Hodgkin's disease. It made him a national celebrity. He followed up this campaign with more weight loss, smoking cessation, stress reduction and get-in-shape programs.

"FIXING" WILTON DRIVE

Shortly after Wilton Boulevard was laid out in 1925, the problems with speeding and parking started, and they still haven't been solved.

In the spring of 1983, a $1.5 million plan was floated to turn Wilton Drive into a shopping area with the ambience of Las Olas Boulevard, Fort Lauderdale's Rodeo Drive (the audience at the council meeting snickered to hear that). Given that more than half the cost was to come from additional taxes on the businesses on Wilton Drive, it failed. It was neither the first nor the last of such plans to go nowhere.

By autumn, it was down to a $1 million project. The city was coming up with $250,000 and the businesses nothing. The plan included left-turn lanes, improved curbs, gutters, sidewalks and irrigated medians.

A year later, it was a $1.25 million project and about to start.

The now $1.4 million project had merchants on Wilton Drive screaming that the construction work in April 1985 was putting them out of business. Meanwhile, the council was trying to get federal funds for a study on how to rejuvenate the businesses along the drive. Some business owners saw this as a move by the city to dictate what color they could paint their storefronts.

Once the project was completed, city hall wanted a celebration. The *Sun-Sentinel* of October 3, 1985, ran a five-column article with a headline: "Completion of Wilton Drive to Be Commemorated in 'Grand Manor.'" The cost was now quoted as more than $1.2 million.[55]

Wilton Drive was described in the article as once having been a twenty-foot-wide dirt road lined by forests. The article goes on:

> *Now it is a five-lane road lined with "mom and pop stores" that cut through the heart of Wilton Manors and join the city to Fort Lauderdale on the south and Oakland Park on the north...*
>
> *At dusk, a fireworks display will cap a day of events that starts with a parade of some 75 units based on a theme that will show the progression of Wilton Manors from a small village in the 1940s to a city with a population of 14,000 in the 1980s.*
>
> *Merchants are planning sales, hoping to regain some of the business that many said was lost when the entrances to their shops were obstructed by construction.*
>
> *A fifth lane for making turns, an improved drainage system, new road surface, better lighting, sidewalks and about 160 new trees are part of the improvements that were completed last week.*
>
> *The appearance and function of Wilton Drive have changed, but the flavor of the road, with its deep-rooted, family-run businesses such as Miller's Hardware and Rothe's gasoline station hasn't seemed to change much at all.*

Frank J. "Cotton" Clinton, age seventy, was selected as honorary marshal for the parade. "The only thing I can think of is I'm so damn old and been around here for a long time. That's the only reason I know of why I was selected." Perhaps he had not been properly briefed. He did remember Wilton Drive when Wilton Manors was still a village and when "the boulevard," as he calls it, was traveled by residents hauling produce from nearby farms to market, Model Ts and the large old Franklin that was driven by former mayor Perry Mickel.[56]

The *Sun-Sentinel* reported in November 1985, more than a month after the project was completed, that the merchants gave it mixed reviews.[57] It also reported that 160 sabal palms and oak trees had been planted.

The state Department of Transportation (DOT) set out to "fix" Wilton Drive again in 1997. Work on the estimated $1.1 million project was scheduled to start in October 1998. It provided better access to The Shoppes of Wilton Manors and measures to prevent shortcuts through residential streets. The headline was: "Wilton Drive Trees May Get the Ax." Most of the trees planted in 1985 were ripped out. DOT regulations say that trees whose trunks were more than three inches thick pose a traffic hazard.

The "rejuvenation" of the drive was again the object of attention with the establishment of Wilton Manors Main Street in 2002. It continues to be the object of attention with a proposed takeover of the road by the city.

CITY MANAGERS

Aside from the city attorney, the city manager is the only city employee who reports to the city commission. All others, including the chief of police, report to him, although the hiring of senior staff must be approved by the commission. The city manager is a full-time administrator, responsible for daily operations.

Since 1960, there have been only eight, in addition to "interim" and "acting," city managers. The latter have typically been senior staff members who have stepped in during times of transition. Lisa C. Rabon, who joined the finance staff straight from college in 1980 and became finance director in 1987, has capably served in this position three times.

The eight permanent city managers have not always had a happy relationship with the city commission, and vice versa. The short tenures of some reflect how critically councils and commissions have viewed the position.

Wally Payne was successful. Robert Levy was visionary but, ultimately, not a good fit.

Joseph L. Gallegos was appointed in 1999. His contract has been extended at least through 2012. The most effective city managers and long-term employees have more than a professional commitment to the city.

In 1984, Marcia Ellington became only the third librarian in the town's history, succeeding Mary Jane Schmidt, who retired after sixteen years. Ellington, who came to Wilton Manors in 1959, joined the library staff in 1968. She oversaw the library's traditional collection of books supplemented by CDs, DVDs and audiobooks. In 1997, the library received a William Gates Grant for public computers. Upgrades and a computer class continue to be popular.

Wilton Manors celebrated its 1985 Fourth of July with the biggest fire in its history. At 3:58 a.m., Florida Power & Light received a call that one of the eight Manor Grove Village condominiums was in flames. Seventy residents of Building H fled, nine of them with injuries. For the rest of the night, Wilton Manors' volunteer firefighters, led by Chief Richard Rothe, fought the blaze that had swept through the attic crawl space and destroyed the building. The cause of the fire turned out to be a short circuit in a storage room.

TWO CONTENTIOUS 1986 ELECTIONS

In September 1985, the political scene exploded again. Council member James Grady (vocal opponent of Cline, Turner and DuBree) resigned from the council to devote more time to his new insurance business, one week before the six-month deadline, which would have allowed the council to appoint a replacement until the following March. Instead, a special election was scheduled to fill the position until Grady's term expired in 1988.

Sherood "Rab" Rouser was appointed to fill the seat until the special election, which had to be called within ninety days. The special election pitted Rouser against Sandy Jedlicka Steen, who had been defeated for council by Cline and Turner in 1982, and Joseph Flaherty, a local business owner.

There was mudslinging.

Steen won, securing her position on the council until 1990, at which time she was elected to the first of two terms as mayor.

In January 1986, the specter of annexation briefly resurfaced, as it had in the 1960s and early 1970s. A group of state senators wanted Fort Lauderdale to annex an unincorporated portion of Broward County. To sweeten the pot, if Fort Lauderdale were to annex Area A, crime-ridden with a very small tax base, it could also have Lauderdale-by-the Sea, Sea Ranch Lakes, Fort Lauderdale–Hollywood International Airport and pieces of Plantation, Lauderhill, Lauderdale Lakes, Tamarac, Davie and Dania.

Wilton Manors was not mentioned, but the idea was floated to merge Wilton Manors with Oakland Park and Davie with Cooper City. The grand plan was to consolidate Broward County to seven to ten cities instead of twenty-eight.[58] One scenario had Oakland Park, Lauderdale-by-the-Sea, Sea Ranch Lakes and Wilton Manors merging.

It did not happen, but economies of scale for the delivery of municipal services have been a chronic problem for Wilton Manors. Over the years, fire-rescue, 911 service and building inspections, as well as the city employees' pension plan, have been outsourced. During the negotiation of the police department's contract in 2006, there was talk about outsourcing police services to the Broward County sheriff, who provides these services for several larger cities. There was a very strong opposition to this idea from Wilton Manors residents.

The ugly March 1986 campaign pitted Mayor DuBree against former ally Vice-mayor Cline and former council member Tracy Stafford. Stafford emerged victorious, with 984 votes to DuBree's 746 and Cline's 520. Richard Mills III, a thirty-one-year-old attorney, and Susan Olson, a thirty-eight-year-old real estate agent, were also elected.

The days of the New Guard, the DuBree faction, the citizen faction and acrimony were over for the time being. They had, however, left their mark.

A GENTLER END TO THE DECADE

It was time for a more up-to-date city logo. We had a contest.

Norma Rollinson, a thirty-year resident and a graduate of the Pratt Institute in New York, won. Her design, created without any city funding, invited visitors with "Welcome to Wilton Manors—Island City" above a drawing of a small island with a healthy stand of palm trees.

Wilton Manors jumps off satellite photos of Broward County as being the "Island City."

Better than a map is a boat trip around the island. The river, narrow at the bridges, is in places two hundred feet wide and sixteen feet deep. Attractive, comfortable homes face much of the waterfront, where residents have planted bougainvillea, magnolias, mangoes, citrus trees and a wide variety of palms. On the North Fork, particularly near the Island City Park Preserve, manatees appear in the winter. Mangroves and cypress grow in the wilder sections of the river. Boats cruising through the waters startle kingfishers, osprey and great blue herons.

In September 1987, Lisa Rabon was appointed as the city's finance director. Wallace "Wally" Payne was hired as the new city manager, a position that he held until 1993.

The city council authorized the largest bond issue in the city's history: $9.6 million to improve the city's water and sewer system. This bond issue was refinanced in 1989.

The latter part of 1987 brought some sadness with the death of John Francis "Jaco" Pastorius III. A graduate of St. Clement School in Wilton Manors and Northeast High in Oakland Park, Pastorius is considered by many to be the

Revolution

greatest bass player who ever lived. Hours after an appearance at the Sunrise Musical Theatre, Pastorius was found unconscious outside the Midnight Bottle Club at 2248 Wilton Drive, now in the Shoppes of Wilton Manors. Witnesses said he tried to kick down the front door and punched the manager/bouncer, Luc Havan, a martial arts expert. In the ensuing fight, Pastorius was badly beaten. He fell into a coma and died six days later. Havan pleaded guilty to manslaughter and was sentenced to two years in jail.

City logo.

Pastorius was acknowledged to have had bipolar disorder and substance abuse problems. The City of Oakland Park dedicated a large park to him in 2008 at 4400 North Dixie Highway.

John Fiore was elected to the city council in March 1988, to what would be the first of three terms. Angela Scott was appointed as city clerk, succeeding Sharon Beerken, who had served for four years. Scott served twenty-one years.

Brian Smith opened his Off Broadway Theater in the former Manor Cinema in 1988 on Northeast Twenty-sixth Street. Producer, director and actor Smith mounted *Papa*, a one-

Lisa Rabon, circa 1980s. *WMHS.*

man play about Ernest Hemingway written by Wilton Manors resident John deGroot. DeGroot was a reporter, editor and writing coach for the *Sun-Sentinel* newspaper. In 1971, he was a member of the team of *Akron Beacon Journal* reporters who earned the Pulitzer Prize for its coverage of the Kent State shootings.

Smith's production starred William Hindman, who had premiered it the previous fall in Miami Beach. The play subsequently made it to Broadway, with George Peppard starring.

Smith's theater brought both eminent performers like character actress Eileen Heckart and outstanding professional South Florida actors. The theater continues today as an auction house.

In 1989, the city let what was probably the oldest house in town slip through its fingers. Horton/Jones Electrical Contractors, Inc., offered to donate to the city the Louis H. Smith house. It was built between 1910 and 1915 for his family at 1225 Northeast Twenty-fourth Street. It appears to be included in the Willingham brochure as "a newly built home in Wilton Manors"—some hyperbole. If this is a picture of the Smith house, it was built long before Willingham's arrival, and it was on the wrong side of the FEC tracks. The house was in disrepair when Horton/Jones bought the property for $67,500 in 1988.

"We wanted it for the land," said Tom Jones. "It was overgrown with trees. You could not see this house when you went down the street."

A year and a half later, needing the land occupied by the old house, the company donated it to the city for possible use as headquarters for the Wilton Manors Historical Society. The city would have to move it. Four years later, the house was demolished after the city failed to take further action.

In the final year of the decade, Bernard Scott stepped down as chief of police after thirty years on the force. The city appointed as its new chief Stephen Kenneth, thirty-eight, who had grown up in the Island City. The son of Fred and Christine Kenneth, he had attended Sunrise Middle School, Fort Lauderdale High School, Broward Community College and the University of Central Florida, earning his degree in law enforcement. In 1973, he joined his hometown police force.

"He knows the city from a perspective that's rare for someone coming in," said Mayor Stafford. "I think he's got a lot of good qualities to bring to that job."

Chief Kenneth would need those qualities. Urban Broward County had grown into a metropolitan area with well over a million people and a daunting variety of problems.

Stephen Kenneth, 1997. *WMHS.*

TROUBLED
ECONOMIC TIMES

The 1990s

Empty storefronts. *WMHS, Photo Contest.*

NEW CENSUS SHOWS CITY FALTERING

Sandra Jedlicka Steen, circa 1990. *WMHS, Steen.*

The numbers in the 1990 census came as an unpleasant surprise. The population was reported to be 11,804, a decline of nearly 1,000 residents. Wilton Manors was not only economically falling behind the rest of Broward County, it was losing population. The Shoppes of Wilton Manors on Wilton Drive were largely empty, with the loss of Stevens Market. The city was not attracting new residents or businesses. The tax base was stagnating, city officials reported. Property owners faced a 26 percent property tax increase in the 1990–91 city budget. The city was fully developed and desperately needed to embark on redevelopment.

Since the amount of funding a city receives from federal and state sources is based in part on census figures, the bad news of a smaller population created additional revenue problems.

Tracy Stafford had resigned as mayor to run for the Florida House of Representatives. He won, becoming the first Wilton Manors resident elected as a state representative, and he served in the legislature for ten years.

Sandra Jedlicka Steen was unopposed in her run to replace Stafford as mayor. She had served on the city council from 1976 to 1982 and from 1985 to 1990.

In an effort to stem the slide, Steen's principal objectives were to continue cleaning up blighted areas and enforcing the municipal codes and ordinances. She was heavily involved in city beautification projects and the Kids in Distress program. In her first term, she was joined by two new council members, Gloria O'Gorman and Richard Pratt. John Fiore was elected vice-mayor. O'Gorman would serve on the city council until 1998 and Pratt until 2000.

In its counterclaim, Wilton Manors asserted that its actual population was two thousand higher. The city persuaded the federal government to add five hundred people to the census total, thus increasing its funding.

In 1991, the Florida Department of Transportation proposed traffic changes at Five Points. A 1987 study, the DOT said, showed that the intersection was confusing and subject to accidents and traffic tie-ups. The plans called for widening Dixie Highway and realigning Northeast Twenty-sixth Street at the intersection.

More than one hundred business owners packed city hall to protest to city council members that the changes would harm businesses. "If it ain't broke, don't fix it," said realtor George Abromats to a round of applause. The council voted unanimously to reject the DOT plan.

The state DOT tried again in 2003, citing the high number of accidents. The DOT had earmarked at least $680,000 for the project. One plan called for the elimination of one of the streets, making it Four Points. Under closer questioning, the DOT said that the improvements would reduce the annual

Five Points: Dixie Highway top to bottom, Northeast Twenty-sixth Street left to right, Wilton Drive, the fifth spoke. The two small towers are visible in the lower left. The other small tower is to the left of the A&W Root Beer stand, which is where the big tower was. Barton and Miller and Reds are at the top, and the Garden Center is at the right. The FEC tracks are at the top right. This picture was taken sometime between 1958 and 1964. *WMHS.*

number of accidents from thirty-three to twenty-seven. It turns out that most of these accidents were sideswipes, and there had been no fatalities during the period studied. Mayor Jim Stork wondered why the state would want to spend this money. "Isn't that about $100,000 per accident?" he asked.[59] The DOT went home, again leaving Wilton Manors with its signature, if challenging, Five Points intact.

In 1991, the Snake Man arrived. Wray Parr and his seventy-two-year-old mother bought a house on Northwest Fifth Avenue in June. In October, Parr arrived from Nova Scotia, Canada, in a converted school bus, which housed about eighteen snakes, including two pythons weighing 100 and 140 pounds.

The neighbors didn't like it. The city went after him on the grounds that it was illegal to park a school bus in a residential neighborhood.

Parr maintained that it was a motor home. The city disagreed. "It looks like a bus; it drives like a bus," said Mayor Steen. "He can register it as a luxury condo, but it's still a bus."

Fines were imposed and suspended. Courts made judgments and suspended them. Tours of the snake hotel were given. Small children were entranced. Parr wound up parking it at a mall in Lauderhill and charging admission to his "serpentarium." This was rerun in one form or another for the next two winters. The feud escalated when the Snake Man gave his

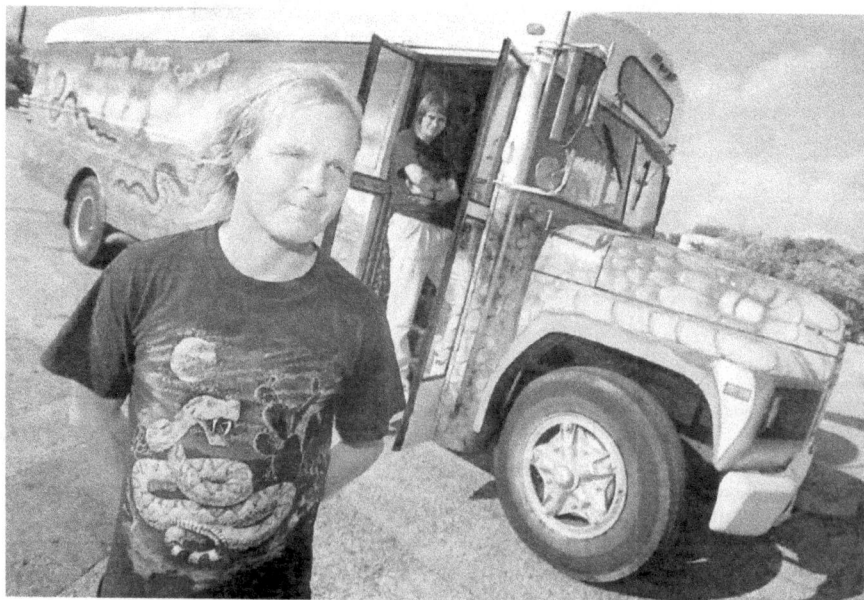

Wray Parr, the Snake Man, 1993. *WMHS,* Sun-Sentinel.

vehicle a $2,000 paint job, in which "a mighty python hovers over a burning Wilton Manors City Hall as rats named after City Council members scurry from the building."[60]

Sources in Nova Scotia confirmed that Parr was "an activist."

"He's a character out of a Stephen King novel," said Harold Horne, the city's community services director. One of the rats had Horne's name on it.

Parr was a master at "tweaking" the city government, merchants, neighbors and anyone who got in his way. The city seems to have been an easy and vigorous target for him.

Tony Barone with Nancy Stafford, circa 1993. *WMHS.*

The feud ended in the fall of 1994, when word came from Nova Scotia that the Snake Man had died of a heart attack. He was forty-four.

In August 1992, Hurricane Andrew struck the southeast coast of Florida. The compact storm's worst damage was in southern Miami-Dade County, but Broward and Wilton Manors also felt its effects. The storm struck the Florida mainland on August 24. By September 1, costs to the city totaled $565,528.

On Veteran's Day, November 11, 1992, the Veteran's Memorial at Hagen Park was dedicated. Anthony J. Barone, a veteran of World War II and Korea had been instrumental in creating the park. Veteran's Day observances are held annually at the memorial, now relocated along Wilton Drive.

In 1993, John "Jack" Seiler was appointed to complete the term of Sue Olson, who had resigned. Seiler would win a four-year term in 1994.

NEW CITY MANAGERS AND A NEW MAYOR

In the summer of 1993, city manager Wallace "Wally" A. Payne and the city parted ways. Payne had been city manager since 1987, when he was appointed

King Wilkinson, 1994. *WMHS.*

Brenda Clanton, circa 2005. *WMHS.*

following turbulence in the city manager's office. His departure brought renewed instability, which lasted until 1995. Lisa C. Rabon, now the city's finance director, capably served as "acting" or "interim" city manager.

King Wilkinson, active in Wilton Manors real estate, succeeded Sandy Steen as mayor in 1994. Born in Casco, Maine, in 1962 Wilkinson moved to Cocoa Beach, where he worked in the space program before becoming a general contractor. In 1967, he moved to Wilton Manors. He won reelection in 1996 and led the city in its fiftieth birthday.

As Wilton Manors neared the end of its first half century, the city turned its attention to enhancing its cultural life and revitalizing its downtown. Brian Smith's Off Broadway on Northeast Twenty-sixth Street had already shown that the area could support a quality theater.

At the beginning of the century, silent films had been made in the area. *Miami Herald* columnist and reporter Carl Hiassen, grandson of Wilton Manors pioneer Carl Hiassen, wrote the novel *Striptease* in 1993. With stars Burt Reynolds and Demi Moore, the book was turned into a movie, with filming taking place throughout South Florida in 1995, largely in Broward County. One location that was needed was a trailer park to serve as the home for hard-luck stripper Erin Grant's fictional sister-in-law.

East of the railroad tracks in Wilton Manors sat the Middle River Trailer Park, which had been owned by Peter Yawt and his family for more than forty years. Just the place for the film crew to work, thought Mayor Wilkinson. The movie's producers agreed.

"It's our funkiest trailer park," said the mayor. "I'm not proud of that, but I'm very proud they did their filming in Wilton Manors." Wilkinson appeared as an extra and enthusiastically promoted Wilton Manors.

Vice-mayor Seiler was dispatched to the filming site and reports that he met Demi Moore, who was wearing a costume he decided not to describe in detail to his wife.

In 1995, Brenda Clanton became the city's human resources director, a position she holds today. She also serves as the city's liaison to the historical society.

TURNING AROUND?

The cultural and economic appeal of Wilton Manors goes far beyond the shooting of occasional movie sequences or part of an episode of *Candid Camera*. Arts and entertainment were a major source of the downtown revival. In 1995, Dr. Robert A. Levy, a Harvard-educated physician, left the position of town manager in Pembroke Park to take on the role in Wilton Manors following Wally Payne. Bob Levy envisioned Wilton Manors as the "Coconut Grove of Broward County" along Wilton Drive.

"Not highbrow," said Levy. "We're looking for cafés and places where ordinary people can enjoy an evening." Art galleries and upscale nightspots were also part of the plans for the city's transformation with an "Arts and Entertainment Overlay District." The district was created in March 1997. The more lenient zoning regulations for businesses along the drive were designed to attract patrons at night. Parking space requirements were relaxed, and it altered the allowable distance between bars. Levy solicited county and state grants for the city's public projects. He lobbied the DOT, pulling in a lot of "chits," to allow a straight shot into the parking lot of the Shoppes of Wilton Manors from Northeast Sixth Avenue, vastly improving the possibilities for the success of enterprises like Georgie's Alibi.

The Arts and Entertainment District reversed the decline, which had been made official by the 1990 census. Broward County and Fort Lauderdale began booming. Wilton Manors became interesting because property values were lower than in surrounding areas and the area was close to downtown Fort Lauderdale. Business and residential investors started to take a second look. They received an especially warm response from community services director Harold Horne, who brokered many redevelopment projects.

Levy left in October 1997 to return to the less-contentious Pembroke Park. Parks and recreation director Daniel Keefe had moved up to assistant city manager when Levy was hired and became acting city manager when Levy left. Richard Rothe had become parks and recreation director in 1995, succeeding Keefe, and William "Bill" Wetzel, a perennial favorite of residents young and old became assistant director.

By the fall of 1997, the effort to attract businesses was bearing some fruit, but much of its future success was tied to converting the 2020 Building, the former Food Fair at 2020 Wilton Drive, into a theater and arts center. The building had been owned by the city since 1977 and leased to Broward County. The Island City Foundation, a 501(c)3 corporation was established, with the city council as the board of directors, to accept

Proposed arts center, 1997. *WMHS*.

funding for the project. The project was slated to be in partnership with the Fort Lauderdale Children's Theatre and the Fort Lauderdale Players. Grants were applied for and planning progressed. Poco French and Paul Kuta were co-chairs of the private fundraising effort. Wilton Manors snagged Joseph Gallegos, former assistant city manager of West Palm Beach, for its new city manager in 1999. West Palm Beach was embarking on perhaps the largest new urbanism/urban renewal project in the state, making Gallegos an excellent choice.

By 2000, the arts project was dead, a victim of spiraling costs, delays and disagreements among the major players. The Island City Foundation, however, continues to fund long-term cultural projects.

The city's fiftieth birthday celebrations in May 1997 were widely publicized and drew attention to Wilton Manors. There was a big parade with Nancy Stafford and Wilton Manors pioneer James Dean serving as grand marshals. Stuart McIver, well-known Florida historian and author, was commissioned to write the history of Wilton Manors on which this book is based.

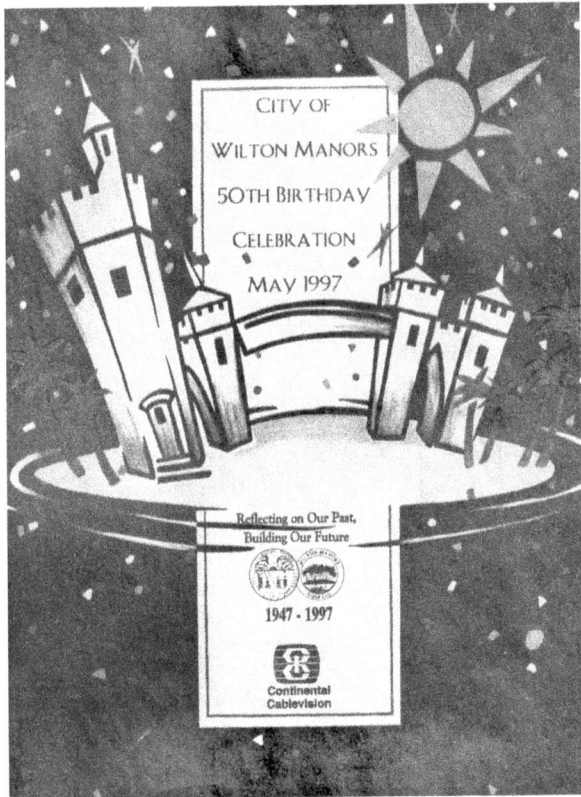

Wilton Manors' fiftieth birthday, 1997. *WMHS*.

137

Ron and Ann Lunsford donated a huge replica of Willingham's Gateway Towers to the city as part of the birthday celebration. Locked away in the model is a time capsule.

With the city's fiftieth birthday celebrations ended in the spring of 1997, focus changed from the past to the future. The political heat was turned up again.

BUILDING MOMENTUM

The election of 1982 was a watershed in establishing the level of professionalism residents expected of their public servants. It took several years for the dissatisfaction on the part of residents to reach a climax. It took several more years to play out.

The pot started to heat up again in the mid-1990s. The issue confronting the city was how to deal with future development and "density" in a geographic area that was quickly running out of buildable land.

In the mid-1990s, the city continued to lose its population and its tax base. Parts of the city were now considered "seedy." The 1990 and 2000 censuses designated Highland Estates as economically depressed. Harold Horne, community services director, reports that when the *Striptease* movie people

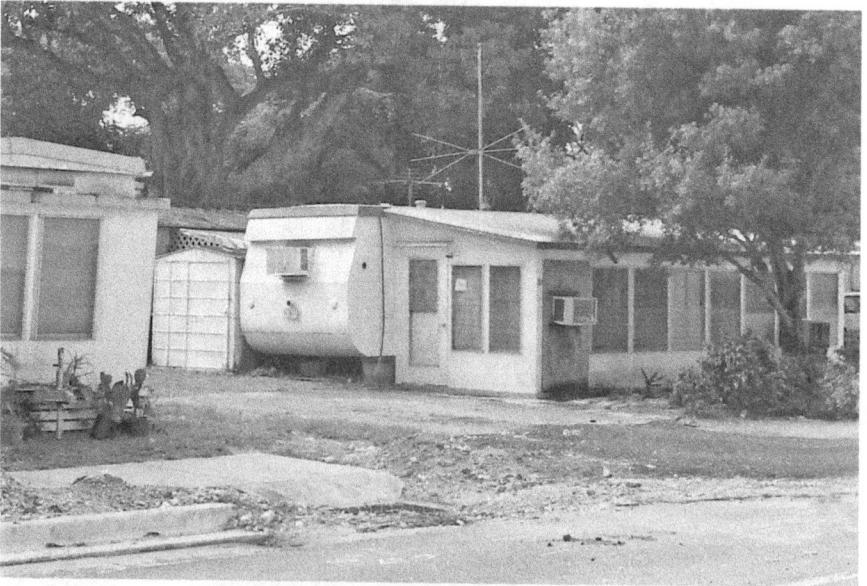

Trailer Haven, circa 1995. *WMHS, Bachman.*

were looking for a trashy trailer park for scenes in the movie in 1995, several trailers had to be painted to appear less trashy.

The stagnant seven-block stretch of Northeast Twenty-sixth Street between Northeast Sixth Avenue and Five Points had been proposed for rezoning to allow businesses in the 1980s. It would be years before this happened. By 1995, the city council was getting more aggressive. It doomed Trailer Haven, which faced Wilton Drive, by prohibiting replacing units. At one time, it had contained gems of little trailers. There was talk of turning it into a museum of trailer life. Some important young families in the history of Wilton Manors had gotten their start there. By the mid-1990s, parts of Trailer Haven suffered serious code violations and crime.

In 1996, the McJunkin family sold a piece of their large, empty landholding in the center of town in the 2200 block of Northeast Seventh Avenue to a developer. The city council gave the developer permission to build some town houses. Wilton Manors needed new development and prosperous new businesses. The town houses were to be more upscale than the surrounding neighborhood, raising everyone's property values. It was suggested that the proximity to Wilton Drive would give it a boost. The newly formed abutting Tropical Pines Civic Association, a neighborhood association, objected to the increased density. It wanted the land to be preserved as a park. Its president, Joanne Fanizza, was a lawyer and chairperson of the city's Board of Adjustment, which had a lot more influence than it does today. She sued the city on the grounds that the zoning variance had not been properly "noticed" to abutters and the public. A Broward Circuit Court judge agreed with Fanizza and the Tropical Pines Civic Association and stopped the project.

The Lines Are Drawn

New political divisions started to emerge between the Old and New Guards. Relations between Mayor King Wilkinson and the rest of the city council became strained when they voted not to reimburse him for legal expenses incurred during an ethics investigation, which cleared him of any wrongdoing. He complained about the decision in the 1996 holiday edition of the city's *Town Crier*.[61]

The March 1998 election signaled a big change. Jack Seiler, vice-mayor, ran against King Wilkinson, who was seeking his third term as mayor. Wilkinson was reported to have underestimated the influence of a growing gay constituency and was perceived as unfriendly to it. Seiler ran an optimistic

Susan, Susanne, Preston, Marianna, Jacqueline and Jack Seiler, 1998. *WMHS, Seiler.*

campaign and was known to be reasonable and open from his previous five years on the council.[62] The *Sun-Sentinel* endorsed him, citing his stabilizing of the city's finances and emphasizing that he was inclusionary and pro-business without subsidizing the private sector. Seiler won by a two-to-one margin.

The council race for two seats attracted seven candidates, including incumbent Gloria O'Gorman. Joanne Fanizza, who had successfully sued the city to stop the development of the McJunkin property on Northeast Seventh Avenue, threw in her hat, as did William Beatty. Diane Cline and James Grady, pivotal members of the council in the early 1980s and who had generally clashed, both ran. Scott Newton, a member of the Planning and Zoning Board, and Gary Resnick, an attorney with a television cable company, rounded out the field.

The *Sun-Sentinel* endorsed O'Gorman and Fanizza. Fanizza and Resnick won. O'Gorman may have been perceived as Old Guard, and it was time for a change. Fanizza was certainly a person of action and had attacked Wilkinson in the campaign. Resnick pounded the pavement, getting out to meet people. He was also openly gay, as was John Fiore, giving credence to the growing gay population.

In 1998, the city council approved the restructuring of the 1989 and 1992 water and sewer bond issues in the amount of $8.1 million to obtain a much lower interest rate (4.33 percent versus 8.8 percent in 1989).

Under Seiler's watch, the Budget Review Committee was formed in 1994 as a check on the council and the city administration. The Annual Island City Canoe Race, which had been inaugurated in 1992 at council member John Fiore's suggestion, became part of the city's birthday celebration every May, and a domestic partnership ordinance was passed.

Troubled Economic Times

A new bond issue for $3.35 million was approved in a November 1998 referendum, $3 million was earmarked to renovate existing parks and purchase land for new parks and $350,000 went to double the size of the library.

Resident volunteer Wayne Schotanus, chair of the Library Advisory Board (appointed by the city commission), helped to place the $350,000 bond issue for the library on the ballot. He subsequently was instrumental in securing a state grant for another $300,000, which tripled the size of the library. Other resident volunteers, led by Paul Kuta, chair of the Budget Review Committee, lobbied hard to purchase the lot and house behind the library to enlarge the footprint of the new building and to provide parking. The Friends of the Library, a separate volunteer organization, established a Capital Campaign Committee chaired by Marlene Schotanus to raise private funds, which provided 80 percent of the money required to furnish the new library when it opened in 2003. Dave Turner had donated the land for the library. Resident volunteers had constructed the original building and provided the labor and funding for its expansion over the years.

Richard C. Sullivan, a longtime city resident who had spent many happy hours in the Wilton Manors Library, died in November 2005. After his death, it was revealed that Sullivan had bequeathed $280,000 to pay the remainder of the library's debt service. On May 9, 2006, the library was renamed the Richard C. Sullivan Public Library of Wilton Manors.

The library continues to be independent of Broward County. It is popular with residents and well supported by volunteers and a professional staff.

The parks portion of the bond issue had mixed results. Parks and recreation director Richard Rothe and his assistant Bill Wetzel worked hard to lay out

Library, 2010. *WMHS, Little.*

David Archacki, circa 2007. *WMHS.*

what park renovations were to be done and where other land might be available for purchase by the city for park use. John Fiore and Joanne Fanizza were the primary drivers on the city council and were supported by Seiler, Pratt and Resnick. Their prime candidates to add to the parks inventory were not for sale, and the funding for other choices did not work out. The city did acquire land to create Donn Eisele Park and expand Kiwanis Park into the Island City Park Preserve. The bond money was also used as leverage to obtain county and state grants, resulting in enhancements to all the parks and the construction of two new community centers.

David Archacki, who had started with the city in 1985, was named director of public services in 1998. This position grew through reorganizations to be director of emergency management and utilities.

The city lost its volunteer fire department in 1999. The selfless volunteers were growing older, and younger firefighters were accepting paid positions with other fire departments. Minimum required skills, such as being a certified paramedic, had been introduced. There were safety issues, and the highly trained, professional mutual aid companies from Fort Lauderdale and Oakland Park had reservations about being under the command of a volunteer force. The volunteer fire department had been a respected entity since the 1940s, and everyone was saddened by its demise. The fire station on Northeast Twenty-second Street is now home to a unit of the Fort Lauderdale Fire Department.

In 1999, Police Chief Kenneth retired, and Assistant Chief Rick Wierzbicki replaced him.

ECONOMIC
ROLLER COASTER

The 2000s

From top: Belle Isle, Wilton Station, The Lofts of Wilton Manors and
Gables Wilton Park, 2010. *WMHS, Little.*

THE ROLLER COASTER GOES UP

If there was a single spark that lit the spectacular growth in Wilton Manors in the 2000s, it was the opening of Georgie's Alibi. George Kessinger and his partners opened a sports and video bar, which catered to a gay clientele, at the Shoppes of Wilton Manors on Wilton Drive in 1997. Georgie's rejuvenated the entire shopping center and began to turn Wilton Manors into a gay "vacation destination." The city began to grow again, with property values rising, vacant storefronts filling up and developers looking for new development. The national census showed Wilton Manors with a population of 12,697, an increase of several hundred over 1990.

Most longtime residents welcomed the increased business activity and the new neighbors who were putting a lot of time, effort and money into their homes. There were new faces on volunteer boards and at city-sponsored events. The outside world may be intrigued with the curiosity of gay mayors and gay majorities on the city commission. Residents are much more interested in a well-run city.

Wilton Manors continues to enjoy an active social scene, including many very well-attended annual and ad hoc city events. The city continues to sponsor the Easter Egg Hunt "Eggstravaganza," a Halloween "Spooktacular," the Christmas tree lighting, Hanukkah and Kwanzaa celebrations with singers and visiting choirs. Residents support the Kiwanis with its sales of Christmas trees and pumpkins. When a neighborhood association undertakes a beautification project, it can count on substantive support from both the Leisure Services and Public Services Departments.

Chardees, a restaurant and bar located where Manors Market once stood at 2209 Wilton Drive, was the first of the gay establishments. Tony Dee (Tony DeRiggi) bought it in 1990 and cleaned it up, bringing in live entertainment every evening and catering to an older crowd. Tropics followed in 1995, in Hagen's old Tropical Club building on Wilton Drive. Seiler went on to run successfully for state representative in 2000, replacing Tracy Stafford. In 2008, he commented that "it was in the 1990s that citizens got invested in the City."

John R. Fiore was elected mayor in 2000. Fiore had served on the Planning and Zoning Board from 1979 until he was elected to the city council in 1988. He was vice-mayor from 1990 to 1992. He was a strong proponent of responsible growth and an advocate for using grant money to improve city facilities.

Fiore's full-time day job was as an urban planner for the Broward County Parks Department. He brought these skills to bear in updating Mickel Field and Colohatchee Park. His skills, perspective and leadership were also important in the reconstruction of Hagen Park and the development of Donn F. Eisele Park and the Island City Park Preserve.

Fiore was Broward County's first openly gay public official. Members of the gay community

John Fiore with his mother, Angela Fiore, Wilton Manors Pioneers 2009, circa 2009. *WMHS.*

had already been attracted to the city, but by 1997, with the opening of Georgie's Alibi, the number of same-sex couples moving in steadily increased. The city's open attitude brought in gays as business owners. By the time Fiore became mayor, property values were soaring. Victoria Park, a depressed area near downtown Fort Lauderdale, had been gentrified by gays in the previous four or five years and had become a very expensive neighborhood. Realtors were now telling prospective buyers that Wilton Manors was the "next Victoria Park." By 2002, they were telling prospective buyers that other neighborhoods in Fort Lauderdale were the "next Wilton Manors."

Fiore's election drew national attention. In the media excitement, Fiore focused on Wilton Manors, telling *George Magazine* in June 2000, "There was no 'gay' agenda...There are no 'gay' potholes."[63] The city, under Fiore's leadership, continued its move up the socioeconomic and social ladder.

Not only gay people were moving in. Because most of the housing stock had been built in the late 1950s and 1960s, homes were small, ideal for single people and small families. Location was also a key attraction.

The 2000 elections made Wilton Manors the second city in the country (after West Hollywood, California) to have a gay-majority council, with the election of attorney Craig Sherritt. June 2000 saw the first Stonewall Street Festival parade down Wilton Drive, an annual event since then.

With a new boardwalk and amenities, Colohatchee Park reopened for the annual canoe race in 2001. On December 13, 2001, ribbon-cutting ceremonies were held for Donn F. Eisele Park, built on land once occupied by the Jenada Pool in Jenada Villas.

John Fiore's tenure as mayor was not smooth. Joanne Fanizza did not support the move to encourage new development with selective zoning for higher-density development. In April 2001, she sued the city again to block the council's decision to allow three two-unit town houses in a neighborhood of single-family homes on Northeast Twenty-first Court. The vote by the council was four to one, with Fanizza being the lone dissenter. This was frequently the case at council meetings, which regularly ran very late. Developers grumbled that Wilton Manors was not a friendly place.

Jim Stork, a thirty-five-year-old entrepreneur, defeated John Fiore in the March 2002 mayoral contest. JoAnne Fanizza placed third. Stork had served on the Budget Review Advisory Committee. His Stork's Café and Bakery, established in 1997 and located in the old Moore's Jewelry store

Groundbreaking at Eisele Park: Craig Sherritt, Joanne Fanizza, Scott Newton, John Fiore and Joseph Gallegos, 2001. *WMHS.*

on Northeast Fifteenth Avenue, was and continues to be a popular gathering place. Both Fiore and Fanizza accused Stork of buying the election. Stork's campaign was positive and looked to the future. This was in strong contrast to Fanizza's opposition to new development and Fiore's perceived lack of vision and energy for the future.

Attorney Ted Galatis won the remaining council seat. Galatis's father was one of James Dean's lawyers, and both his parents are Plantation pioneers. Seiler had set the stage. Fiore had done much of the legwork, and the city started to bloom under Stork. Stork welcomed new investment and encouraged citizen involvement.

Jim Stork, 2002. *WMHS, Stork.*

By the summer of 2002, workers had started removing trees and demolishing the old Hagen Park community center, and the library expansion was proceeding.

The Wilton Manors Historical Society was relaunched as an independent entity in 2002, following periods of activity and dormancy since 1975. It had, as part of the U.S. bicentennial celebration in 1976, produced a number of oral histories, as researchers interviewed many of the people who had been influential in the 1940s and 1950s. The society also republished a pamphlet on the city's history to 1955.

The city had been talking with the Richardson family about acquiring the Richardson House and 5.4 acres of land, the remains of the Richardson Golf Course. Judge Richardson agreed to sell the estate to the city for use as a public park for $3.8 million. In early July 2002, the Broward County Commission approved matching funds of about $1.9 million. Grants from the state of $1.6 million, and a commitment from the city for $300,000, rounded out the purchase price of $3.8 million. Plans were completed for a nature walk, floating dock, pavilion

Photo illustration of Richardson Historic Park and Nature Preserve, 2010. *WMHS.*

and parking. Exotic vegetation was removed, and more grants were applied for.

The city had long outgrown the space for offices and equipment to manage its infrastructure. For some time, it had been leasing space at 2100 North Dixie Highway from the Pioneer Cement Company. This 2.87-acre, triangular piece of land was sandwiched between Dixie Highway and the FEC tracks, the northern point being at Northeast Twenty-fourth Street. This is the approximate location of the center of the Colohatchee settlement. In 2003, the city purchased this land for $2.1 million and relocated both the Public Services and Community Services Departments there, freeing space in city hall and the maintenance yard behind city hall.

In 2004, Jim Stork decided to move up from mayor to run for E. Clay Shaw's seat in the U.S. Congress and announced he would not seek reelection in Wilton Manors. His run for Congress was derailed by the discovery of a heart ailment.

BLOOMING

Donald Scott Newton Jr. defeated Joe Grano, a political newcomer, in the mayoral contest in the 2004 election. Newton, married and the father of three, had the strong support of Stork and the endorsement of the *Express*, a newspaper serving Broward County's gay community. He won by a landslide.

Joseph Angelo was elected to fill the vacancy on the council, becoming the first openly gay African American to hold elected office in Florida. In the next two years, it was nearly impossible to attend a public event in town without seeing Scott Newton and his wife, Cindy. He was reelected in 2006 with 80 percent of the vote.

In March 2004, residents approved a change in the city charter, making the city council the city commission.

An article in the *New York Times* in May 15, 2004, described Wilton Manors as a "gay Mayberry." It said that "Wilton Manors is to urban revitalization what *Will and Grace* was to prime-time television."[64] While appreciative of the attention, to most residents, this was not a big deal.

With the retirement of parks and recreation director Richard Rothe and library director Marcia Ellington in 2003, the city manager combined the

The Newtons: Scott, Cindy, Stephanie, Patrick and Staci, 2006. *WMHS, Newton.*

two entities into a new Leisure Services Department. Patrick Cann was hired as the new department's director in March 2004, with Richard Sterling as library director appointed in April.

In August 2004, the Northeast Twenty-sixth Street bridge to Federal Highway was named for James Dean, who had been instrumental in its construction. Longtime community services director Harold Horne retired and was replaced by Wayne Thies in October.

The city hired Dhillon Management Company, management consultants, in early 2005 to evaluate the efficiency of the police department and to pinpoint the reasons for its escalating costs. The consultants identified a number of problems, including leadership and unchecked spending. As a result, Chief Rick Wierzbicki announced his retirement. Assistant Police Chief Elizabeth "Liz" Gribbon became acting chief.

Rumors abounded that the city's police services would be outsourced to the Broward Sheriff's Office. City commissioners assured residents that the city would not give up its police department.

After a national search, Richard Perez, a commander in the Fort Lauderdale Police Department, was selected from a pool of eight finalists to serve as the city's eighth police chief, starting in January 2006.

In April 2005, Cynthia A. Thuma, author of a number of books on South Florida history, published *Images of America: Wilton Manors*, a pictorial history of the city.

Hurricane Wilma hit South Florida on October 24, 2005. While not one of the biggest or most destructive hurricanes in recent history, it assembled just the right combination of elements to knock Wilton Manors off its feet. With Hurricane Rita earlier that year, the easy stuff got hit. Fences blew over; tree limbs came down. With Wilma, water sloshed in the toilet before the water supply gave up completely for a couple days. Two weeks after the storm, about half of Wilton Manors was still without electricity. Roofs were gone; huge trees were pushed over. Longtime residents had a hard time finding their way around town. "I turn right at the big red sign." The sign was not there. "I pass this stand of trees and take a left." The trees were not there.

Neighbors helped one another with clearing yards and stood in line for gasoline, water and ice. They made new friendships and renewed old ones. Power was restored piecemeal over two or three weeks. In 2004, the city had contracted with an outside company to provide emergency cleanup services. Its services were used for Hurricane Frances in 2004 and Katrina in 2005. It picked up eleven thousand yards of debris for Katrina and six

Hurricane Wilma aftermath, 2006. *WMHS, Photo Contest.*

times that amount for Wilma! Managing the cleanup (and documenting FEMA requirements) and performing ongoing city business for the six weeks following Wilma proved extremely difficult for the city. It has now contracted with experts to manage the cleanup for the next hurricane.

A volunteer citizens group led the charge in the fall of 2005 and the spring of 2006 to approve a $6 million bond referendum for a new municipal complex to include a city hall and police station. It passed overwhelmingly.

Voters also changed the date for the local elections from March to November, beginning in 2008, giving incumbents an extra eight months in office.

Planning for the new government complex was no less difficult than what the city had gone through in the 1950s when the old city hall was built. There were questions about its location and its design. In the spring of 2008, an extremely well-attended and energetic meeting was held at Hagen Park Community Center. Residents made their wishes known. Loudly. The city commission listened.

Mayor Scott Newton was reelected in March 2006. The city commission approved the $1.3 million purchase of the quarter-acre property housing Rothe's Garage, which was established in 1957 at 2128 Wilton Drive, to provide additional space for the new city hall complex.

On May 10, 2006, the Wilton Manors Civic Association disbanded, sixty years to the day from when it was originally formed. It had been founded to allow nonelected citizens to provide volunteer support to the city. In the early 1980s, it found new life as a forum, often political, to effect big changes in how the city government was run.

By 2006, it had been replaced with myriad organizations, including the commission-appointed Planning and Zoning Board, the Recreation Advisory Board, the Board of Adjustment, the Budget Review Committee and the Community Affairs Advisory Board. These joined the active Westside Association of Wilton Manors (WAWM), the Central Area Neighborhood Association (CANA) and the Eastside Neighborhood Association (ENA).

Wilton Manors Main Street, Inc., was formed in 2002 as an alliance between the city and business owners, primarily on Wilton Drive, to encourage new businesses and upgrade the drive. Its design committee, headed by Brett Nein, longstanding member of the Planning and Zoning Board, published design guidelines to give renovations and new construction a unified vision.

On November 26, 2006, Wilton Manors was declared by the National Wildlife Federation (NWF) the seventeenth city in the nation to be a Certified Community Wildlife Habitat. This honor was the result of citizens landscaping with bird- and butterfly-friendly Florida plants and registering their yards with the NWF. M.E. DePalma was relentless, preaching to friends, neighbors and public meetings on the virtues of returning the land to the real "Florida." She held classes and lobbied to earn this distinction for the city. In 2009, the city dedicated a park in her name, complete with a large bronze butterfly.

POSITIONING FOR THE FUTURE

The groundbreaking ceremony for the Richardson Historic Park and Nature Preserve took place on February 23, 2007. Judge George Richardson Jr., whose father had bought the property in 1938 to construct a golf course, was the guest of honor. Invasive species of plants had been removed, grants had been secured and plans had been made to make this the jewel in the crown of Wilton Manors. With the groundbreaking ceremony, work began in earnest on the grounds and structures.

Serious new construction had been underway since 2003. On Wilton Drive, the key word was "mixed use"—retail on the first floor, residences above. Belle Isle, a town house mixed-use development on Wilton Drive, replaced Trailer Haven. The homes facing Wilton Drive have retail space on the ground floor. The $80 million Wilton Station multi-building condominium complex replaced the Wm. Thies & Sons beer distributor complex at Five Points. There is retail space facing Northeast Twenty-sixth Street. The Gables of Wilton Manors was approved in 2007. It has 145 residential units and nineteen thousand square feet of commercial space. It replaced a strip mall that contained Wilting Manners, Pearce's 5 & 10, Liberty Embroidery, Marsupium, About Town Lock and Safe and Kelly's Classics, along with other businesses. The retail space on the ground floor includes an office for Wilton Manors Main Street. Wilton Cove, a development of about 20 nearly million-dollar homes was built east of Northeast Seventh Avenue and Northeast Twentieth Street.

James Dean's old house, later Secord Funeral Home and then Spectrum House, has been replaced by the Island City Lofts, an impressive structure, again with retail space on the ground floor and loft condominiums above.

Highland Estates, which had been designated an "economically depressed area" in the 2000 census, has been in-filled with upscale town houses and lofts.

Another $9 million bond was issued in 2007 to undertake new utility-related projects and refinance the 1989 and 1998 water and sewer bonds.

The Wilton Manors Baptist Church became the NorthStar Community Church. Mayor Hal Price's Pure Oil service station on Wilton Drive had become Wings and Things, a favorite for buffalo chicken wings with locals. By 2007, Wings and Things was gone, to be replaced with an ambitious project that failed before completion in the bad economy.

In 2008, Gary Resnick, a commissioner since 1998, was elected mayor and was joined on the city commission by newcomers Justin Flippen and Tom Green. The spring of 2009 saw the completion of Snook Creek Park on Powerline Road and the South Fork of the Middle River.

In 2008, the Gay and Lesbian Community Center (GLCC) in Fort Lauderdale purchased 5.6 acres of land with four buildings from Global Crossing Satellite Communications Company at 2040 North Dixie Highway. In 2009, the GLCC renamed it the Pride Center at Equality Park. It joins Kids in Distress, whose large complex has been on Northeast Twenty-sixth Street since 1992, and the PACE Center for Girls, on Andrews Avenue since 2002, as important nonprofit support organizations whose reach extends far beyond Wilton Manors.

By the summer of 2009, the exterior of the Carriage House at Richardson Park had been restored, with paint and labor donated by the Ed French Painting Company, a second-generation Wilton Manors family-owned company. The Broward Trust for Historic Preservation gave the city an award for its efforts. The nature trail, boat dock and furnishings in the Manor House were complete.

Pride Center at Equality Park, 2011. *WMHS, Little.*

The official grand opening for the Manor House was held on July 23, 2009. At age ninety, George Richardson Jr. participated in the ceremonies, as he had participated in the 2007 groundbreaking and ribbon-cutting for the park. He died eight days later, on July 31, 2009.

The new city hall, police department and Emergency Operations Center officially opened in January 2010, taking the 2020 Wilton Drive address of the notable edifices previously located there. The old building, which had long outlived its usefulness, was torn down, and the space returned to much-needed parking. A longer-term solution to "the parking problem" continues to be discussed.

The City Commission after the November 2010 election in the new City Hall: Scott Newton, Vice Mayor Tom Green, Mayor Gary Resnick, Julie Carson and Ted Galatis, November 2010. *WMHS, Winslow.*

ANOTHER 1926 HOUSING BUBBLE?

Wilton Manors was front and center in the housing bubble in the mid-2000s. Architecturally unremarkable homes from the 1950s and 1960s were turned into gems—a pool here, French doors there, a tiny piece of the Amazon jungle in the front yard all went a long way. The granite countertop and stainless appliance salespeople got rich. Houses were flipping faster than pancakes at IHOP. Happily, many of the new residents stayed, and the city was infused with a new generation of activists, volunteers and good neighbors.

Just like 1926, the market crashed, but it did so on a national and even international level. It was deeply painful to watch neighbors lose the homes they were upside-down on. We snuck onto the rapidly deteriorating "bank-owned" properties to cut the weeds down to something resembling a lawn.

The value of property increased by 124.5 percent between 2000 and 2007, reaching a total of $1 billion. It subsequently declined by 35.8 percent between 2008 and 2011. The population also declined by about one thousand between 2000 and 2010.

The boom created a lot of very fine housing stock, particularly in Highland Estates. The great promise also created a lot of mixed-use, residential retail space on Wilton Drive and Northeast Twenty-sixth Street. Unhappily, some of it did not come to fruition. Several buildings look to be abandoned, and there continue to be empty storefronts. Various volunteer organizations and the city are aggressively attacking the problem. The history of Wilton Manors suggests that an aggressive attack by concerned citizens will end in success.

"Jack" Seiler, former Wilton Manors council member, Wilton Manors mayor, state representative, Fort Lauderdale mayor and always good friend to Wilton Manors, was asked in 2008 what made Wilton Manors unique. He cited the high level of volunteerism and involvement:

> *Being an "Island City" sets us apart, as does our physical size and population, but it is the investment in the community, going back to our earliest days and which continues to the present with the active neighborhood associations, the City advisory boards, the Main Street organization, the independent Library, the Kiwanis Club, the Historical Society, the active participation of citizens at City Commission meetings, and events like the Annual Canoe Race and Taste of the Island which make us unique.*

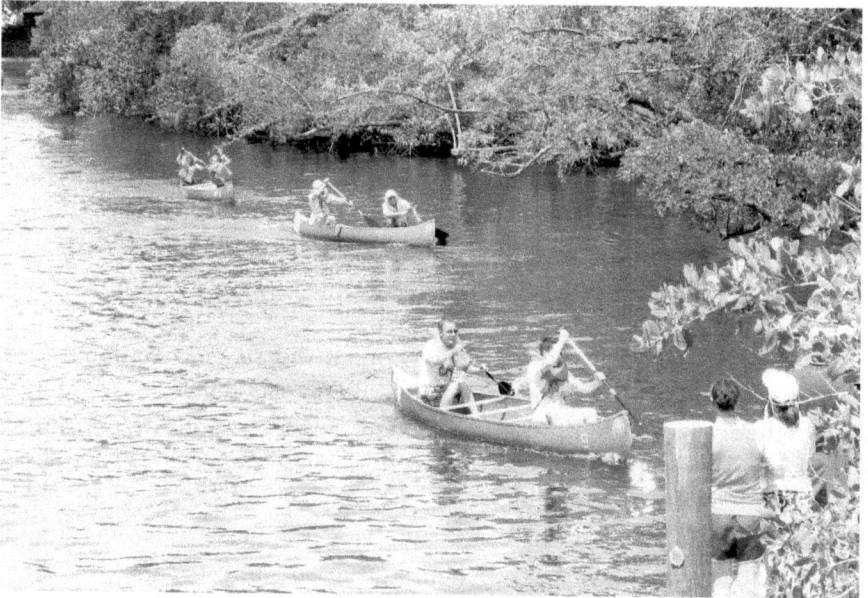

The Island City Annual Race to Circumnavigate Wilton Manors in a Canoe: One Hundred Years of Building a Community. *WMHS, Little.*

Economic Roller Coaster

Willingham set off in boom times that turned bad. This cycle has repeated itself numerous times in the last eighty years and will continue to do so into the future. Wilton Manors has an army of people determined that it will succeed. In the 1940s and 1950s, there was only a handful of movers and shakers. Today, there are scores, selflessly giving of their time and expertise to make Wilton Manors the best.

Wilton Manors is proud to be the "Island City." Two square miles. With just about twelve thousand residents. Embraced by the North and South Forks of the Middle River!

PHYSICAL GROWTH

Wilton Manors plats. *WMHS, Little, Official Broward County Records.*

More detailed information on the physical growth of Wilton Manors may be found at the historical society's website: www. wiltonmanorshistoricalsociety.org.

BEFORE WILLINGHAM

The Spanish were the first European settlers in what would become Florida, arriving early in the sixteenth century. The Spanish, French and English aligned and realigned themselves with various Native American tribes for two centuries of very bloody battles. In 1763, Spain traded Florida to England in exchange for Havana, Cuba. This made West Florida and East Florida the fourteenth and fifteenth colonies. West Florida extended from the Mississippi River east to the Apalachicola River. The capital was Pensacola, and the northern border shifted a number of times. East Florida had a capital at St. Augustine. Both colonies remained loyal to England during the War of Independence, and the 1783 Treaty of Paris returned them to the Spanish. The Spanish presence was small and easily overwhelmed by settlers from the new United States. Florida was also a haven for escaped slaves and a launching pad for Native American attacks.

In 1821, the Floridas were acquired by the United States in a treaty with Spain. Florida became a state in 1845. The Swamp Land Act of 1850 transferred land unfit for cultivation—because it was "swamp"—from the federal government to various states. It was to be drained and cultivated. Today, the swampland to be "fixed" under this act would be preserved as wetlands. The Florida state legislature put the responsibility "to provide for and encourage a liberal system of internal improvements"[65] on five trustees of the Internal Improvement Fund of the State of Florida. This led to the huge effort to drain the Everglades.

In 1889, the State of Florida agreed to grant land to the Florida Coast Line Canal and Transportation Company in exchange for the construction of a canal from St. Augustine to Biscayne Bay. Land was to be granted based on satisfactory inspection of work that had already been completed. In September 1890, a large piece of land, including all of what is now Wilton Manors, was given to the canal company.

The canal company, chronically short of cash, sold $1.4 million worth of bonds secured by its land to the American Loan & Trust Company of New York in 1888. The bank went bankrupt in 1891.

In direct competition with the canal companies, Henry Flagler and the Florida East Coast Railway Company were also being granted substantial amounts of land from the trustees of the Internal Improvement Fund for construction of the railroad until the action was declared illegal. Taking advantage of the canal company's financial difficulties, Flagler purchased so much land from it that he created several companies to deal specifically with land, including the Model Land Company.

In 1896, the Model Land Company bought twenty-five thousand acres, including the land in Wilton Manors, from the canal company.

The first "settlement" was focused on Northeast Twenty-fourth Street at the FEC Railway tracks. There is strong evidence of a train station there as early as 1894 and as late as 1926. The Colohatchee Woman's Club, the Smith House, Johnson's Farm, the train stop and a little convenience store clustered around Northeast Twenty-fourth Street and the FEC tracks; all predated Willingham and formed clearly a "center of activity."

W.C. Kyle and Earl Hendrickson and their wives bought 120 acres from the Model Land Company in August 1924. They quickly sold it in March 1925 to Willingham. Willingham also bought "Uncle Billy" Johnson's farm along the west side of the FEC tracks. Presumably, others who had sold to Willingham had also acquired their land from the Model Land Company.

BEFORE INCORPORATION AS A VILLAGE: 1925–1946

Willingham was not the first to plat land in what is now Wilton Manors. In 1910, Colahatchee, Florida, was platted by F.R. Oliver, T.C. Moody and S.H. Weaver. In May 1910, George M. Phippen platted a subdivision that appears to have contained twenty-four lots. It was also called Colahatchee. On March 18, 1925, H.C. Jelks and his wife, Beula, platted Beulaland west of Andrews Avenue. There were several small subdivisions platted in 1925 and 1926 along Northeast Twenty-fourth Street east of the railroad tracks.

On June 11, 1925, Willingham filed an official plat for Unit 1, Wilton Manors, for E.J. Willingham Development Co. J.S. Rhine was the civil engineer who prepared the plat. It was signed by Willingham; his wife, Eula; his son E.J. Willingham Jr. and his son's wife, Viola; and his daughter, Mary, and her husband, W. Ross Chambers.

Wilton Manors stretched from the FEC tracks and Dixie Highway on the east to Northeast First Avenue on the west. The northern boundary was Northeast Twenty-sixth Street. The southern boundary was Northeast Twentieth Drive and Northeast Twentieth Street to Wilton Boulevard, north a block to Northeast Twenty-first Street, west a block to Northeast Third Avenue and then west another block on Northeast Twenty-first Court to Northeast First Avenue. It was about 345 acres.

Ambitiously laid out but marked "Not Included" was the land south of Northeast Twentieth Street and Northeast Twentieth Drive to a canal and what would become Townhouse Isle to the South Fork of the Middle River. It picked up land south of the South Fork of the Middle River (which is now part of Fort Lauderdale) and went west to Andrews Avenue. There was a series of canals in what is now Richardson Park and Manor Grove Condominiums, providing waterfront lots. Willingham's residence was at the southwestern end of Wilton Boulevard.

Willingham Sr.'s Wilton Manors failed. His son, E.J. Willingham Jr., replatted Wilton Manors in May 1928. Wilton Boulevard became Wilton Drive, and most of the Indian names were replaced with numeric designations. The new plat actually "un-subdivided" the property, removing most of the individual home sites. Only much larger parcels of one and a half to over four acres each remained, which would have made them easier to sell to developers.

About twenty-eight lots were excluded from the re-subdivision, retaining the original plat descriptions. These had possibly been sold by this time. The Hiaasen House, on the corner of Northeast Twenty-first Court and what was

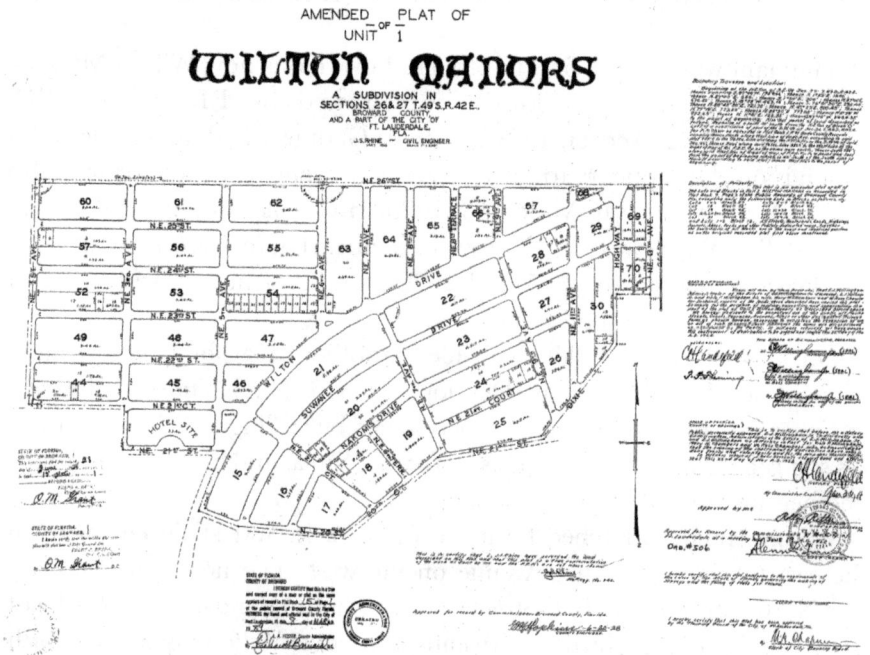

Wilton Manors, Unit 1, amended by E.J. Willingham Jr., 1928. *WMHS, Official Broward County Records.*

renamed Nakomis Drive, was one of these lots. Others were scattered primarily around the edges. All of the north side of Northeast Twenty-third Street between Northeast Fifth Avenue and Northeast Sixth Avenue, just off Wilton Drive, were excluded, hinting at the start of a village center.

There are no plats recorded during the Depression of the 1930s. Those who could afford to pay the back taxes on foreclosed properties increased their landholdings. John P. Pedersen was able to lay claim to being the largest landowner in Fort Lauderdale in this manner. His purchases included land in Wilton Manors.

In 1945, Dave Turner is reported to have bought all previously unsold lots—some 238 parcels—from the Willingham estate for $12,500. This area must have composed the majority of the Willingham plat. In 1947, he recorded a plat for about 83 parcels, which would have composed about one-third of his 1945 purchase.

In 1946, Al Hagen added thirty-four parcels to the Wilton Manors area by platting the subdivision of Wilton Manors First Addition. This was a roughly pie-shaped area north of the Willingham/Richardson property, west of Wilton Drive to Northeast Twentieth Street.

1947 INCORPORATION BOUNDARIES

The village of Wilton Manors was incorporated in 1947. It stretched from the FEC tracks on the east and Northeast Twenty-sixth Street on the north to the South Fork of the Middle River on the south. The western boundary was twelve hundred feet west of Andrews Avenue (Northwest Fifth Avenue). It did not include the Richardson Golf Course or Lazy Lake but did include all of Willingham's original plat. On April 28, 1947, the Broward County Circuit Court accepted Colonel William J. Robinson's petition from the Civic Association to incorporate.

The next set of subdivisions recorded for Wilton Manors were all signed by the mayor and clerk of the village council.

DEVELOPING FROM THE CENTER

April 19, 1951, saw the single largest increase in the size of Wilton Manors when voters agreed to annex all the land east of the FEC Railway between the North and South Forks of the Middle River. This increased the size of the village by about 80 percent.

Except for a short corridor on Northeast Twenty-fourth Street just east of the FEC tracks, most of the area had not yet been platted. Farming was limited to the farm and dairy belonging to Earl L. Middleton. He had moved to Wilton Manors with his family in 1944, and the thirty-five-acre farm and dairy had belonged to the Charles Mahannah family some thirty years earlier. Middleton owned a jewelry store in downtown Fort Lauderdale and was president of that city's chamber of commerce. He also served on the Wilton Manors Village Council from 1951 to 1953 and again from 1954 to 1958.

In December 1951, voters decided to annex the land along both sides of the FEC tracks between Northeast Twenty-sixth Street and the North Fork of the Middle River. Known as Middleton Gardens, it extended to the west side of Dixie Highway. This annexation included zoning the area for commercial or industrial use. After extended debate, residents approved use of the property by Maule Industries, a cement company. At some point, "no taxes" would end, and taxes paid by the plant would help reduce the anticipated burden on the citizenry. Today, Wilton Station, a large condominium complex, is located on the former Maule Industries property.[66]

In August 1951, Wilton Manors once again added a large portion of land. Newspaper accounts often referred to this addition as "the annexation of Highland Estates," but it included all the land east of Andrews Avenue, south of the North Fork of the Middle River and north of Northeast Twenty-sixth Street to a couple blocks west of Dixie Highway. The actual Highland Estates subdivision was east of Northeast Sixth Avenue.

In general, Highland Estates had much larger and deeper lots than those south of Northeast Twenty-sixth Street. Many wound up with two little houses on them, one behind the other, or small apartment buildings at right angles to the street.

In the 1940s, Highland Estates was all residential and was loosely governed by its Civic Club, which had a building on Northeast Eighth Avenue. It also had a small volunteer fire company with one truck based on Northeast Sixth Lane and a water distribution system with water obtained from Oakland Park. There were periodic discussions about the civic merger of Highland Estates and Wilton Manors. In 1946, Highland Estates formally voted against joining Wilton Manors. Residents feared the usurpation of its assets by Wilton Manors and being subjected to the

HIGHLAND ESTATES

A SUBDIVISION IN SEC 26-TWP 49 S - RGE 42 E
BROWARD COUNTY, FLA
PAUL E. DYE-OWNER & DEVELOPER

Highland Estates plat, 1940. *WMHS, Official Broward County Records.*

latter's strict zoning and other regulations. Both entities, however, feared having to pay taxes for Fort Lauderdale's increasing debt burden.

In 1950, Wilton Manors residents still obtained their water from wells. As the village grew, this became increasingly unacceptable, and the village council began to look for a solution.

The big questions to answer were: with whom should they contract to supply the water and how should they pay for a water distribution system? The first overtures to Fort Lauderdale as a water supplier failed. Discussions between village attorney Colonel Robinson and Oakland Park eventually resulted in a water supply contract signed in February 1952. In August 1951, Wilton Manors authorized a $75,000 bond to pay for the construction of a water distribution system; the bond would be repaid by fees on the resale of water to its residents. Wilton Manors also arranged to pay Highland Estates $5,000 for its water distribution system. In July 1952, the Sunset Manors residential subdivision on Northeast Twenty-sixth Street west of Northeast Sixth Avenue was the first to receive water directly from Oakland Park. Wilton Manors now receives its water from Fort Lauderdale.

With the water issue between Highland Estates and Wilton Manors settled, on August 7, 1951, residents voted overwhelmingly for the latter to be annexed into the village of Wilton Manors, increasing the population of Wilton Manors by 350, or about 110 families.

The development of the east side was primarily the result of the efforts of Dave Turner and Jim Dean, aided by several prominent Fort Lauderdale developers.

Dean and a number of other businessmen underwrote building a four-lane dirt road that became Northeast Twenty-sixth Street east from Five Points in 1952.

Access from Federal Highway and Fort Lauderdale was critical to the Fort Lauderdale investors who were starting to take an active interest in the area. James Dean persuaded developers to put up the $20,000 required to build a bridge as a private initiative. On December 20, 1952, the bridge was dedicated and given to Broward County. In August 2004, this bridge was named in honor of James C. Dean.

Middle River Estates, Coral Point, Coral Gardens and Coral Estates were platted. Middle River Manor and Edgewater Estates provided waterfront properties with long canals, reaching nearly to the south side of Northeast Twenty-sixth Street.

Although Dean and Turner had financial interests in a variety of real estate developments, their names often were hidden behind various legal corporations. Turner later donated land and money for the establishment of the First Christian Church on Northeast Fourteenth Avenue; Dean donated the land for the Wilton Manors Kiwanis Club at the north end of the street, just east of the FEC tracks.

Physical Growth

Jim Dean led the way for commercial development with the Manor Gate Shopping Center. By the end of 1957, the development of Eastern Wilton Manors was complete. Dean, however, was unable to pull off locating the new city hall at Manor Gate Shopping Center, in spite of offering to donate the land to the city.

John U. Lloyd wanted the east side of Northeast Sixteenth Avenue north of Northeast Twenty-sixth Street in his Middle River Estates rezoned as commercial. After three tries with the city council, he gave up in the summer of 1957. His lawyer and friend, state senator Ted Cabot, introduced a bill in the legislature for the dis-annexation of these ten acres. It passed, but Governor LeRoy Collins vetoed it at the last minute, keeping Wilton Manors intact.

In January 1951, John P. Pederson and his wife, Lillian, submitted an amended plat for Sunset Manors, between Andrews Avenue and Northeast Sixth Avenue. This large area was part of the Highland Estates annexation.

In February 1952, F. Thomas Amato and his wife, Anna, submitted a plat for Amadale, east of Highland Estates and west of Dixie Highway. The Babcock Company of Fort Lauderdale platted the Amadale Addition in February 1955. Neither plat was signed by the City of Wilton Manors, and these two subdivisions were, in fact, not part of Wilton Manors.

The development of land west of Andrews Avenue progressed more slowly than it did elsewhere in the city and continued through 1968. On March 18, 1925, H.C. Jelks and his wife, Beula, platted Beulaland, Northwest Twenty-fourth and Twenty-fifth Streets between Andrews Avenue and Northwest Third Avenue. The subdivision saw little activity and contained only two houses in 1946, when Bob and Nancy Sawallis built the third house there. Perry Mickel's son, Robert, confirms that the Clark house on Northwest Twenty-fifth Street behind Hamel Tire was built in the 1920s.

West of Andrews Avenue is about 380 acres, mostly farmland or uncultivated land. Major landholders were Perry Mickel, with about 55 acres, and S.B. Sullivan, with 100 acres. Roads, if any, were unpaved.

In the late 1940s, the Andrews Avenue extension through Wilton Manors was paved, greatly aiding north–south travel. Perry Mickel and his wife, Dorothea, platted Mickel's Second Addition to Wilton Manors in 1950. Over the next six years, the Mickels either platted and developed their western land or sold it to others.

The June 26, 1952 edition of the *Wilton Manors Bulletin* reported that the council suggested annexation of all the property west of Andrews to the Seaboard Railroad and north to Oakland Park Boulevard.

By 1955, the North Fork of the Middle River, which had wandered northwest across Oakland Park Boulevard at Andrews Avenue, had been channeled into Canal C-13, extending west along the south side of Oakland Park Boulevard. This extension by the South Florida Flood Control District eventually linked the South and North Forks of the Middle River. This is how Wilton Manors became the "Island City."

The entryway walls on either side of Northwest Twenty-ninth Street at Northwest Seventh Avenue marked the entry to Jenada Villas, a subdivision that crossed Powerline Road. They were built by Robert Lubbers, who was the maternal grandfather of Wilton Manors mayor Scott Newton. These walls have been restored by the Westside Association of Wilton Manors (WAWM) as a signature piece for that section of the city.

In July 1959, the plat for the exclusive Jenada Isle residential development was filed. Jenada Isle was the last major development on vacant land in the city. A gated community, it represented the "high end" of Wilton Manors. Much of it was developed by Jens Rask, and twenty-six of the eighty-one properties were designed by noted architect Paul M. Bradley Jr., who still lives in the subdivision.

Both River Terrace and River Ranches are located north of the North Fork of the Middle River, as is half of Almar Estates. Their northern border is Oakland Park Boulevard. River Terrace was annexed as a result of city-requested state legislation. The re-subdivision of River Terrace was added in 1961. With the annexation of these two subdivisions, Oakland Park Boulevard serves as the northern boundary of Wilton Manors from Northeast Sixth Avenue to the Seaboard Railroad to the west.

TOWNHOUSE ISLE

"'Outdoor Living Room' Is Planned With Each Home" was the headline in the April 28, 1962 *Fort Lauderdale News*, announcing that ground had been broken on Townhouse Isle, along the South Fork of the Middle River, east of Wilton Drive. There were to be 13 two-story buildings, each with six to twelve units, for a total of 110 town homes, 76 of them on the water. The land had been owned by Alvar Hagen. After the September 1947 hurricane, he had gone to the Northeast Fourth Avenue bridge and measured a foot above the high water, figuring that this would be the minimum he would need for fill. Prices ranged from $14,950 to $24,950. The homeowners' association was the Townhouse Isle Club, Inc. One had to apply to the club

Photo illustration of Townhouse Isle as it might have looked in the 1960s. *WMHS, Little.*

for a certificate of membership prior to negotiating a purchase "to insure the compatibility of all residents."[67]

During construction, there was access from Wilton Drive on Northeast Nineteenth Street, but after completion, the only way on or off the island was over the newly constructed bridge at Northeast Seventh Avenue and Northeast Twentieth Street.

Looking at Willingham's original plat, Townhouse Isle was clearly part of his vision. The "Isle" has grown substantially over the years, with a number of separate homeowners' associations, a variety of architectural styles and a couple of freestanding homes. Townhouse Isle maintains its fierce independence. After Hurricane Wilma in 2005, the homeowners' associations talked with the city about obtaining assistance in cleaning up the streets blocked by a number of large, old trees. After considerable pressure from many communities, FEMA finally agreed to pay to clean private streets that were not part of a gated community and where the U.S. Mail and school buses regularly operated. The city offered to take over the streets after Wilma. The homeowners' associations rejected the idea.

THEY GOT AWAY

The March 1957 election included a referendum on annexing Lloyd Estates and the Sleepy Acre subdivisions, north of Oakland Park Boulevard, and areas north to Northwest Thirty-ninth Street. At this time, the North Fork of the Middle River crossed Oakland Park Boulevard at Andrews Avenue and continued northwest, making this area a logical addition to Wilton Manors. Attempts to annex these areas failed.

ACKNOWLEDGEMENTS

The Wilton Manors Historical Society Board of Directors has provided unswerving support for this effort over a number of years. It continues collecting, interpreting and clarifying our history. It has opened interesting new paths, down which may lie volume two:

Diane Renollet Cline, President
Cynthia A. Thuma, Vice-President
Paul A. Kuta, Treasurer
Benjamin B. Little, Secretary
Doris E. Cotnoir, Director
Shirley A. Nolen, Director
Mary Gayle Ulm, Director
Ronald A. Ulm, Research and Technology Chair
Jonathan Heller, Former Director
Ann Lunsford, Former Director
Patsy Staletovich, Former Director

Diane Cline personally made a great deal of the history reported in this book. She has generously offered clarifications and additional facts. She has made no effort to enhance history's view of her. She is too busy continuing to make history.

Director Mary Gayle Ulm, with her co-chair of the society's research committee and husband, Ron Ulm, has relentlessly unearthed incredible new information on the earliest days of Wilton Manors and corrected many myths. Mary has delicately opened doors to some of the original players; children of the original players, now in their eighties; and people who were here in the early days. In the process, she has harvested important new facts and subtle nuances and blown away much conventional wisdom. Mary took incredible amounts of data about the physical growth of Wilton Manors and made it intelligible. Unhappily, we have had to truncate that here, but it is available in whole on the Wilton Manors Historical Society website. Ron has offered solid advice and backed it up with solid technological support, including the monumental task of organizing all the pictures.

Paul A. Kuta's clear thinking and organizational skills have had a significant impact on the clarity of this work. His encyclopedic knowledge of the comings and goings of the last several decades has been a tremendous help, as have his insights as "a player."

Cynthia A. Thuma's unpublished update to Stuart McIver's 1997 history was the jumping-off point and inspiration for this work.

The current and past city commissioners have provided important moral and financial support to this effort. They carry the torch lit by the "founding fathers" ninety years ago:

> Gary Resnick, Mayor
> Thomas Green, Vice-mayor
> Julie A. Carson, Commissioner
> Ted Galatis, Commissioner
> Scott Newton, Commissioner
> Joseph Gallegos, City Manager

City staff, led by City Manager Joseph Gallegos, has been key to unlocking hidden treasure. Staff members have been patient and responsive to requests for information. Former city clerk Angela Scott and current city clerk Kathryn Sims, along with Assistant City Clerk Patricia Staples, have unearthed important primary documents. Finance Director Lisa Rabon and Human Resources Director Brenda Clanton, who is the city liaison with the Historical Society, have provided clarifications, context, content and perspective.

Director of Leisure Services Patrick Cann unfailingly supports the efforts of the historical society. The Leisure Services staff has provided the historical society with hundreds of photos of city events.

The watercolor on the front cover was painted at Richardson Park by noted Florida artist Toni Sailer. It depicts the west façade of the Manor House flanked by Royal Palm trees. The painting was purchased through personal donations of senior staff of the City of Wilton Manors Leisure Services Department and gifted to the Wilton Manors Historical Society. The watercolor is on permanent display in the Manor House. In turn, Ms. Sailer transferred exclusive rights to the image to the Wilton Manors Historical Society—in support of its role in the development and preservation of Richardson Park.

Joan Kon, police department records manager, shared her history of the police department and her research material. Chief Wierzbicki and Chief Perez were very generous in sharing their archives and photos.

We are particularly grateful to the following people. They have patiently sat for interviews. They have patiently provided clarifications. They have generously searched their archives for photos. They have provided insights into life in Wilton Manors far beyond a recitation of facts and dates. Some of their specific contributions are noted in the photo credits and the endnotes:

Mary Jo Eakin, daughter of Lamar Braddy
Joyce Hagen Horner, daughter of Alvar Hagen
Gwen Mace King, one-time resident of The Towers
Robert Mickel, son of Perry and Dorothea Mickel
George Richardson Jr. and his children, founding family
Nancy Sawallis, longtime resident
Shirley and George Schneider, daughter and son-in-law of John Pedersen
Ginger Pedersen, granddaughter of John Pedersen
Marcia Stafford and her son Tracy and daughter Nancy, all major players
Gwen Thompson and the Woman's Club of Wilton Manors
Magdeline Robbins Thuma, longtime resident

The Broward County Historical Commission, county historian Helen Landers, archivist Denyse Cunningham, Mary Rose Harding and administrator Dave Baber have been most supportive, as have the Fort Lauderdale and Oakland Park Historical Societies.

A major thank you to Dr. Jena Gaines for her patience and understanding in editing this work and providing the author with a level of confidence necessary to continue.

Appendix
CIVIC CHRONOLOGY

WILTON MANORS CENSUSES

1950	883
1960	8,257
1970	10,948
1980	12,742
1990	11,804
2000	12,697
2010	11,632

MAYORS

Dave Turner, April 28, 1947–March 3, 1952

Perry Mickel, March 3, 1952–November 2, 1955

J. Frank Starling, November 2, 1955–January 12, 1960

Harold T. Price, January 12, 1960–January 31, 1968

Marvin Meecham (acting), January 31, 1968–March 12, 1968

Gerald F. Thompson, March 12, 1968–July 18, 1974

James E. Maurer, July 18, 1974–October 8, 1975; March 1980–1984

Eugene Metzger, October 14, 1975–March 9, 1976

Arthur Welling, March 9, 1976–March 1980

Robert DuBree, March 1984–1986

Tracy Stafford, March 1986–1990

APPENDIX

Sandra Jedlicka Steen, March 1990–1994
King Wilkinson, March 1994–1998
John P. "Jack" Seiler, March 1998–2000

John Fiore, March 2000–2002
Jim Stork, March 2002–2004
Donald Scott Newton, March 2004–2008
Gary Resnick, Nov 2008–

CITY COUNCIL/COMMISSION MEMBERS

Alvar Hagen, 1947–1952
Arthur Chabot, 1947–1952
William Robinson, 1947–1952
J. Marvin Brown, 1947–1952
James Boyd, 1947–1952
James Creighton Dean, 1952–1953
Earle Middleton, 1952–1953, 1954–1958
J. Frank Starling, 1952–1955
Earl Gurney, 1952–1954
Charles Saxer, 1953–1955
Clarence Riggs, 1953–1956
George Richardson, 1954–1956
Fred Stevens, 1955–1958
William Joslin, 1955–1958
Vernon Burnell, 1956–1960
Harold T. Price, 1956–1960
Robert Schmidt, 1958–1960
Carl Blimly, 1958–1961
Howard Goll, 1959–1962
Gerald McCulley, 1960–1964
George Nichols, 1960–1963
John Hanrahan, 1960–1965
Marcia Stafford, 1961–1975
William E. Smith, 1962–1974
Gerald Thompson, 1964–1968
Lawrence Sullivan, 1966–1968
Marvin Meacham, 1965–1971
Eugene Metzger, 1968–1974

James Maurer, 1968–1974, 1979–1980,
Arthur Welling, 1971–1976
Samuel Stevens, 1974–1979
Fred B. Fetzer, 1974–1979
Wayne Goltz, 1974–1976
Tracy Stafford, 1975–1981
Sandra Jedlicka Steen, 1976–1982, 1985–1986, 1988–1990
Jack R. Zeman, 1976–1984
Michael B. Curren, 1970–1984
James Maurer, 1979–1980
James Grady, 1980–1985
Donn Eisele, 1981–1982
Diane R. Cline, 1982–1986, 2008
William Turner, 1982–1986
Loren "Duke" Maltby, 1982–1984
Sherod "Rab" Rouser, 1985
Marvin Bush, 1984–1988
Wayne Musgrave, 1984–1986
Susan Olson, 1986–1993
Richard Mills III, 1986–1990
John Fiore, 1988–2000
Gloria O'Gorman, 1990–1998
Richard Pratt, 1990–2000
John P. "Jack" Seiler, 1993–1998
Joanne Fanizza, 1998–2002
Gary Resnick, 1998–2008
Donald "Scott" Newton Jr., 2000–2004, 2008–

Civic Chronology

Craig S. Sherritt, 2000–2008
Ted P. Galatis Jr., 2002–
Joseph M. Angelo, 2004–2007

Julie Carson, 2007–2008, 2010–
Justin Flippen, 2008–2010
Tom Green, 2008–

CITY MANAGERS/ADMINISTRATORS

J. Frank Starling, 1960–1981
Tracy Stafford, 1981–1982
J. Scott Miller, 1982–1985
Bernard S. Scott, 1985 (acting),
1986 (acting)
Dale Reith, 1986
Laura Z. Stuurman, 1986–1987
(acting)
Wallace A. Payne, 1987–1993

Lisa C. Rabon, 1993 (acting)
Richard L. Black, 1993 (interim)
Donald Lusk, 1993–1994
Lisa C. Rabon, 1994–1995 (interim)
Robert A. Levy, 1995–1997
Daniel W. Keefe, 1997–1999
(interim)
Lisa C. Rabon, 1999 (interim)
Joseph L. Gallegos, 1999–

CITY CLERKS

Kathryn Johnson, 1947–1950
Mary Harvey, 1950–1952
Marcia Stafford, 1952–1960
J. Frank Starling, 1960–1978
Dorothy Grosser, 1978–1979
Margaret Mitchell, 1979–1980

Debbie Bassone, 1980–1982
Deanne J. Doherty, 1982–1984
Diane Hominick, 1984
Sharon Birken, 1984–1988
Angela Scott, 1988–2009
Kathryn Sims, 2010–

POLICE CHIEFS

Richard Beaney, 1952–1957
Thomas Brace, 1957–1961
Harold Gair, 1961–1966
Felix Miller, 1966 (acting)
Bernard S. Scott, 1966–1989

Stephen Kenneth, 1989–1999
Richard "Rick" Wierzbicki, 1999–
2005
Elizabeth Gribbon, 2005 (acting)
Richard A. Perez, 2006–2010

VOLUNTEER FIRE CHIEFS

C. Kass, 1952
Ed Novak, 1952–1953
Ed Thomas, 1953–1954
Wallace Wakely, 1954–1959
Al Walker, 1959–1960

John S. Miller, 1960–1980
Richard Rothe, 1980–1995
James Ridout, 1995–1997
Tim Keefe, 1997–1999

PARKS AND RECREATION

Leisure Services Directors

Harry Davis, 1955–1960
James Bernard McGivern, 1960–1963
Richard Geisler, 1963–
Robert Saxon

Cecil Nall, 1983–1984
Daniel W. Keefe, 1984–1995
Richard Rothe, 1995–2004
Patrick Cann, 2004–

NOTES

BEFORE WILTON MANORS

1. Cooper Kirk, "The Vanished Communities of Broward County," *Broward Legacy* (Summer/Fall 1991): 20.
2. Mark Mahannah, interview by Cooper Kirk, tape recording, May 15, 1982, Broward County Historical Commission, Fort Lauderdale, FL.
3. Kirk, "Vanished Communities," 20.
4. Paul S. George, "In the Beginning: The Origins of Oakland Park," *Broward Legacy* (Winter/Spring 1992).
5. *Fort Lauderdale City Directory*, 1920–21.
6. *Fort Lauderdale Sentinel*, "Does Fort Lauderdale Want Pompano's Aid?" January 15, 1915, 6.
7. *Fort Lauderdale Sentinel*, "County Division Far from Being a Dead Issue," January 8, 1915, 2.
8. Stuart B. McIver, "Touched by the Sun." In *The Florida Chronicle*, Vol. 3 (Sarasota, FL: Pineapple Press, 2001.
9. Kirk, "Vanished Communities," 28.
10. Everglades Digital Library, "Reclaiming the Everglades: South Florida's Natural History, 1884 to 1934," Everglades biographies, Richard "Dicky" J. Bolles. Biography prepared by Gail Clement, Florida International University, adapted from Alfred Hanna and Kathryn Hanna, *Lake Okeechobee, Wellspring of the Everglades* (New York: Bobbs-Merrill Co., 1948).
11. *Fort Lauderdale Sentinel*, July 30, 1920.

12. William J. Northern, ed., *Men of Mark in Georgia*, Vol. 6 (N.p.: A.B. Caldwell, Publisher, 1912).
13. "Mrs. Willingham Expires at Home," Riverside Cemetery of Macon, Georgia, riversidecemetery.com (accessed December 17, 2007).
14. Philip Weidling and August Burghard, *Checkered Sunshine: The History of Fort Lauderdale, 1793–1955* (Gainesville: University of Florida Press, 1966).
15. Deed restrictions from warranty deed between E.J. Willingham et al and Carl A. Haissen, dated October 31, 1925.
16. Virginia Rogers, "Wilton Manors Topics," *Fort Lauderdale News*, 1956.
17. Harold Price, "Wilton Manors Was Born in 1924," *Fort Lauderdale News*, May 27, 1965.
18. Rogers, "Wilton Manors Topics."
19. *Fort Lauderdale Sunday News*, January 30, 1926.
20. "Interview with Carl Hiaasen by Cooper Kirk," September 28, 1984, Broward County Historical Commission, Oral History.
21. Donald W. Curl, "Boca Raton and the Florida Land Boom of the 1920s," Tequesta Digital Files #XLVI, 1986.
22. Norman Malcolm, "Early History of Wilton Manors—Early Developers," *Wilton Manors Bulletin* 2 (August 1951).

THE FOUNDING PIONEERS

23. Robert Mickel, interview by Mary Gayle Ulm, May 2009, Wilton Manors, Florida.
24. Gex and Betty Williams, "The Early Days," *Island City Gazette*, Special Pioneer Days Issue, September 17, 1989.
25. Estelle W. Culmer, "Wilton Manors, An Incorporated Suburb," *Broward Sunday Sun*, November 21, 1948, sec. C.
26. Shirley and George Schneider, interviewed by WMHS, May 9, 2009.

THE VILLAGE OF WILTON MANORS

27. "'Secession' Plans Revealed at Council Meeting at Manors," *Broward Sun*, October 21, 1948.
28. Estelle W. Culmer, "Wilton Manors: An Incorporated Suburb," *Broward Sunday Sun*, House and Home, November 21, 1948.

29. Ibid.

30. Ibid.

31. Mary Jo Eakin, interviews by Mary Gayle Ulm, May and June 2011.

32. *Wilton Manors Bulletin*, "Food Fair Super Market to Build in Village," July 17, 1952.

33. *Wilton Manors Bulletin*, "Christmas Committee Chairman Names Additional Members," November 20, 1952, 1.

34. *Wilton Oakland Sun*, "Pool Is Badly Needed, City Fathers Admit," August 13, 1953.

35. *Wilton Manors Bulletin*, "Village Attorney Robinson Gives Water Question History at Mass Meeting," February 28, 1952.

THE CITY OF WILTON MANORS

36. Carter Holmes, "Hot Air," *Wilton Oakland Sun*, February 26, 1953, 1.

37. *Wilton Oakland Sun and Coral Ridge Revu-er*, "New Wilton Manors Council Split Wide Open," November 12, 1953.

38. Ibid.

39. Virginia Rogers, "Wilton Manors Topics," *Fort Lauderdale News*, January 12, 1956.

40. Ibid., November 30, 1956.

41. *Wilton Oakland Sun*, "10,000 Is Voted To City Hall Fund," December 10, 1953, 1.

42. Rogers, "Wilton Manors Topics," July 12, 1957.

43. Ed Magill, "Boos City Officials," *Fort Lauderdale News*, May 22, 1957.

44. Rogers, "Wilton Manors Topics," July 1957.

BUILDING OUT

45. Elizabeth Baier, "John Miller. 'Coach' of Manors Fire Department," *South Florida Sun-Sentinel*, online edition, January 24, 2007.

REVOLUTION

46. Jeff Forgoston, "Manors Mayor Calls Appointment an Illegal One, Suggests Probe," *Fort Lauderdale News*, January 10, 1979, 4B.

47. Lori Alessi, "Manors Civic Group to Name Officers," *Tribune*, November 18, 1981, 7.
48. Robyn Feldman, "Manors Fires Veteran Attorney," *Fort Lauderdale News*, March 17, 1982, 3B.
49. Joseph Cosco, "Fall of Political Ax Shakes Up Wilton Manors," *Fort Lauderdale News*, August 31, 1982.
50. Hank Selinger, "Mayor's Absence Baffles Manors," *Miami Herald*, July 1, 1983.
51. Chris Cubbison, "Manors Mess Proves Need to Get Serious," *Miami Herald*, June 30, 1983.
52. *Sun-Sentinel*, "Dubree, Bartels, Grady, Howells recommended," March 6, 1984.
53. Ellen Stein, "Manors Petitions Force Opposing Ballot Questions," *Sun-Sentinel*, October 4, 1984.
54. Ellen Stein, "Musgrave Ousted from Manors Council," *Sun-Sentinel*, November 11, 1984.
55. Ellen Stein, "Completion of Wilton Drive to Be Commemorated in 'Grand Manor,'" *Sun-Sentinel*, October 3, 1985.
56. Ibid.
57. Doreen Wood, "Not All Wilton Drive Merchants Are Pleased with Road Repaving," *Sun-Sentinel*, November 11, 1985.
58. Jeffrey Moore, "Officials Reject Proposal for Annexation Poll," *Sun-Sentinel*, January 31, 1986, 1-B.

TROUBLED ECONOMIC TIMES

59. Daniella Aird, "Manors Resists 5 Points Plan; Leaders, Residents Oppose Removing One of Its Streets," *Sun-Sentinel*, May 15, 2003.
60. Jennifer B. Heit, "Snake Charmer," *XS Magazine*, December 8, 1993.
61. Jennifer Heit, "Critics Malign Mayor Comments in Manors Newsletter at Issue," *Sun-Sentinel*, December 22, 1996, 3.
62. Lisa J. Huriash, "Wilton Manors Mayor Ousted," *Sun-Sentinel*, March 11, 1998.

Economic Roller Coaster

63. *George Magazine*, June 2000.
64. Ginia Bellafante, "Newest Gay Mecca Is Less of Key West, More of Mayberry," *New York Times*, May 15, 2004.

Physical Growth

65. Acts of 1855, Chapter 610, General Statutes of Florida, 1906, Sections 616, 617 and 620.
66. *Wilton Manors Bulletin*, November 7, 14, 21 and 28, 1951.
67. *Fort Lauderdale News*, "Development Under Way," April 28, 1962. Quote from Charles N. Sumwalt Jr., president of Townhouse Development Corp.

BIBLIOGRAPHY

NEWSPAPERS

Broward Sunday Sun
Florida Sun-Sentinel [Fort Lauderdale]
Fort Lauderdale News
Fort Lauderdale Sentinel
Island City Gazette, Special Pioneer Days Edition, 1989
Miami Herald
New York Times
Wilton Manors Bulletin
Wilton Oakland Sun
XS Magazine

COLLECTIONS

The Broward County Historical Commission Collection
The Broward Legacy
The Everglades Digital Library, FIU
Florida Chronicle
Riversidecemetary.com
Wilton Manors Bulletin

BOOKS AND MANUSCRIPTS

Harrell, Carolyn. *Kith and Kin.* Macon, GA: Mercer University Press, 1984.

Kon, Joan. "Historical View of the Wilton Manors Police Department." Unpublished report, August 11, 2001.

Malcolm, Norman. "Wilton Manors Background: Early History." Unpublished manuscript in the collection of the Wilton Manors Library, 1948.

McIver, Stuart B. *The Island City: The Story of Wilton Manors.* Wilton Manors, CL: Published by the City of Wilton Manors, 1997.

Thuma, Cynthia. *Images of America: Wilton Manors.* Charleston, SC: Arcadia Publishing, 2005.

INDEX

ABOUT THE AUTHOR

B enjamin Little grew up in a family of scholars and historians in Concord, Massachusetts. He went into computers. A degree in drama from Tufts University (requiring Shakespeare instead of an English major's Chaucer) was followed with course work toward an MA in architectural history and an MBA. The computer work concentrated on how to make things work in a business environment, not the ones and zeros.

The editorship of a condominium newsletter sharpened both his reportorial skills and his ability to document the absurd. His first book was a compilation of reminiscences of thirty college students in their junior year in London in 1968–69. The next was a series of essays and genealogical data about his mother's family, who arrived in Newbury, Massachusetts, in 1635. The next projects will include the memoirs of a distant cousin, Louise B. Graves (1867–1964), a never-married and well-traveled woman whose father was a failed preacher, failed businessman, failed art collector, failed father and failed husband but a successful trout fisherman.

Mr. Little finally reconciled 350 years of New England heritage with two feet of snow on the car every time he returned from Florida and moved to Fort Lauderdale full time in 1996. He found his way to Wilton Manors in 1998.

He puts in an occasional appearance at city commission meetings, where he sometimes generates some chuckles, as well as some very uncomfortable squirming by selected elected or appointed officials.

The contributions to this work by members of the Wilton Manors Historical Society Board of Directors cannot be overemphasized. Cindy

Thuma grew up here. Ron Ulm grew up across the river. Mary Ulm arrived with Ron from Atlanta in 2002 upon their retirements. Mary can most often be found in the trenches, doing spectacularly competent, important and unglamorous work. Diane Cline has been here and making history—or at least trouble—since 1977. Paul Kuta retired here in 1996 and has been in the thick of it since.

www.ingramcontent.com/pod-product-compliance
Lightning Source LLC
Chambersburg PA
CBHW070357100426
42812CB00005B/1543